PMS (PREMENSTRUAL SYNDROME)

Barbara Moe

The Rosen Publishing Group, Inc.
New York

Published in 1998, 2002 by The Rosen Publishing Group, Inc.
29 East 21st Street, New York, NY 10010

Copyright © 1998, 2002 by Barbara Moe

Revised Edition 2002

All rights reserved. No part of this book may be reproduced in any form without permission in writing from the publisher, except by a reviewer.

Cover photo © Index Stock

Library of Congress Cataloging-in-Publication Data

Moe, Barbara A.
Coping with PMS / Barbara Moe.
p. cm.
Includes index.
Summary: Discusses the causes and symptoms of premenstrual syndrome and what sufferers can do to treat it.
ISBN 13: 978-1-435-88776-3
1. Premenstrual syndrome—Juvenile literature. [1. Premenstrual syndrome.] I. Title.
RG165.M638 1998
618.1′72—dc21

97-38630
CIP
AC

Manufactured in the United States of America

Introduction	1
1 The Female Body	3
2 Ovulation and Menstruation	18
3 PMS	26
4 Lifestyle Changes	41
5 Do You Need More Help?	77
6 Self-Help, Psychotherapy, and Support Groups	93
7 Healthy Recipes for Busy Young Women	105
Glossary	129
Where to Go for Help	133
For Further Reading	136
Index	138

Introduction

The poster shows a black cat with frazzled fur and a menacing look. She says, "I have PMS and sharp claws. Any questions?"

A birthday card features a picture of a cake slashed with a hatchet. "Some Special Advice for the Birthday Girl," it reads. Inside is the warning: "Never cut your cake during PMS."

How about the story of the bakery with a mean owner. The high school kids in the neighborhood called it "The PMS Bakery."

And finally, have you heard this PMS "joke"? A man asks a woman with premenstrual syndrome: "Why does it take four women with PMS an hour to change a lightbulb?"

She clenches her teeth, makes hissing sounds, and replies, "Because it does. OK?"

Legends, stories, and jokes about premenstrual syndrome (PMS) abound. PMS is a combination of physical and emotional symptoms that occurs before menstruation begins. If you're a young woman with PMS, you may or may not think it's funny to make light of your condition.

Coping with PMS (Premenstrual Syndrome)

No one knows exactly how widespread PMS is, but most people believe it's very common. Some experts estimate that 90 percent of all women suffer from PMS at one time or another. Others say that as many as 50 percent have it regularly, and for at least 10 percent of women PMS is severe enough to disrupt their lives. Some say premenstrual syndrome affects all women but that some women do not notice it because it's not that severe.

In spite of today's advances in medical technology, scientists have not found a simple cure for PMS. It's not like other illnesses. If you have a sore throat, you go to the doctor and he or she does a throat culture. If the germ streptococcus is the culprit, your doctor will probably prescribe an antibiotic. Twenty-four hours later, you're feeling better.

No simple treatment exists for PMS. What works for one person may not work for another. A good idea may be to experiment with the suggestions in this book and find out what works for you.

The Female Body

Some women are proud of their bodies and know how to take care of them. Others know little about their own bodies and are embarrassed to talk about them. Learning about your body is one way to start appreciating it. Learning about menstruation is the beginning of caring for yourself and your own health needs. It's important to know the anatomical (scientific) terms for your female parts. Then when you go to a doctor, you will be more comfortable talking about your body and you'll know the right questions to ask.

Puberty

The rapid growth that you experience during puberty is called a growth spurt. In sixth or seventh grade, you may begin to notice that most of the girls are taller than the boys. That's because girls get their growth spurt—the first sign of puberty—at about the age of ten, and boys don't get theirs until a couple of years later. Before puberty, both boys and girls grow about two inches a year. Once puberty hits, you can grow as much as four inches in a year. By the time you get your first menstrual period, your growth will probably have slowed down. By the second or third year after your first period, you will probably have stopped growing completely, though it is possible to grow another inch or two up to the age of twenty-one or so.

Growing taller is only one of many changes that occur during the growth spurt and puberty. But what makes puberty start in the first place? In girls between the ages of eight and fourteen, nerve cells in the hypothalamus (part of the brain) send signals to the pituitary gland to release hormones that affect the ovaries (the reproductive organs that hold all the eggs you were born with). These hormones signal your ovaries to increase production of the female sex hormones, estrogen and progesterone. It is the increase in these two hormones that triggers all of the changes in your body during puberty.

There are a lot of changes that take place in just a few years. Overall, your body will become more curvy. This is mainly because your hips and thighs will broaden and your pelvis will expand. Your body fat is rearranged during puberty, so new fat tissue grows around your abdomen, hips, thighs, and buttocks. This is to get your body ready for a possible pregnancy. This is a normal and healthy process; it does not mean you are getting fat. To carry a baby someday, your body needs to be more solid in the middle than it was when you were a kid.

Your breasts will also begin to get bigger. The area around your nipples grows first, and then your breasts get bigger and rounder until you are eighteen or so. You may worry that your breasts are too large or too small. Don't compare yourself to others because each girl's rate of growth and size is different.

The Female Body

While your hips and breasts are filling out, your face will probably become thinner. Your features will become more distinct as the bones in your face change. Your feet will grow faster than the rest of your body, including your arms and legs. This may make you feel a little awkward, as if you're always tripping over your own feet. But don't worry; the rest of your body will soon catch up.

Puberty also causes hair to grow in new places, such as around your genital area (your private parts). About a year after this hair appears, you will also begin to notice hair under your arms. At the same time, the hair on your legs will grow thicker and may become darker. The hair on your arms may also darken.

You will also notice that you begin to sweat more during your teenage years and that the sweat has more of an odor than it used to have. This is because your sweat glands are more active. You can avoid body odor by showering often and by using a deodorant or an antiperspirant.

The oil glands in your body are also more active during adolescence. Overly active oil glands can cause skin problems. Pimples, blackheads, and whiteheads form when oil is trapped in the pores of your skin. They are signs of acne. Acne occurs in three out of four teenagers. It can usually be treated with nonprescription products. But in serious cases, acne may need to be treated by a doctor.

You may feel like you no longer recognize your body. Talking to your friends about what is happening will help you feel better. Together, you can discuss how your bodies are changing and how that makes you feel. You will realize that you are all experiencing the same sort of confusing, exciting, and sometimes frightening changes, and you can support each other through this difficult time.

Coping with PMS (Premenstrual Syndrome)

On the other hand, you may be worried because your body hasn't started to change yet while your friends' have. Every girl is different and will develop at her own rate. In addition, sometimes extremely athletic girls, such as gymnasts, experience a late puberty. If you are worried that you are developing slowly or late, consider talking to your mother or another adult about when she went through puberty. Chances are you will begin puberty at about the same time your mother did. But don't worry; it will happen.

Hormones

Hormones are chemical substances that carry messages from one organ to another organ or to other tissues in your body. A variety of sex hormones work together to start up, maintain, and eventually discontinue your monthly reproductive cycle, or menstrual period. It is thought, though it has not yet been proven, that the monthly fluctuations in the levels of female sex hormones are at least partly responsible for PMS symptoms, including mood changes.

The two major female sex hormones are estrogen and progesterone, which are produced mainly by the ovaries. Another hormone, the follicle-stimulating hormone (FSH), is produced by the pituitary gland (located at the base of your brain). FSH stimulates the follicles that surround the eggs in your ovaries. This stimulation causes the production of estrogen. When estrogen levels become high enough, a part of the brain called the hypothalamus signals the pituitary gland to release luteinizing hormone (LH). When LH levels hit their peak, the ovary releases an egg and also produces progesterone.

The Female Body

All of these hormones work together to build up the lining of the uterus. If the egg becomes fertilized by a man's sperm, a pregnancy may result. If the egg is not fertilized, progesterone levels begin to drop, and the lining of the uterus (the endometrium) breaks up and causes bleeding. This is menstruation, your monthly flow of blood. When estrogen and progesterone levels drop after menstruation, FSH gets produced, and the cycle begins again.

Genes

Genes are the building blocks of heredity. They determine most of your physical features as well as some personality traits and whether you are predisposed to certain medical conditions, such as premenstrual syndrome. If your mother had PMS, it doesn't mean you'll definitely have it, but you may be more likely to get this condition than would a person whose mom did not have PMS. Experts suspect that a genetic link exists to premenstrual dysphoric disorder (PMDD), a severe and debilitating form of PMS. Women with a personal or a family history of mood disorders, such as depression and postpartum depression (the "baby blues"), seem to be at a greater risk for developing PMDD.

Knowing Your Own Body

Years ago, a group of eleven women wrote *Our Bodies, Ourselves: A Book by and for Women*. Many times updated since its first publication, this pioneering book came out of the women's movement of the 1960s. It may have been one of the first works to suggest that a woman can and should use a mirror to observe her own sexual organs.

The female sexual organs (sometimes referred to as reproductive organs because of their role in producing a baby) are outside as well as inside the body.

Breasts

In girls between the ages of ten and twelve—the onset of puberty—girls' breasts usually begin to grow and assume a rounded shape. When they get to the size your genes intended them to be, they will stop growing. If they grow a lot, you may wish they were smaller. If they don't grow "enough," you may wish they were bigger.

The dark saucerlike area on the outside of your breasts, in the middle, is called the areola. The small raised area in the middle of the areola is the nipple. (Some nipples are indented and some are flat—all variations are normal.) Bumps on the areola of some women's breasts are oil glands that protect the nipple when a woman is nursing. Some women have a few hairs around the areola. That too is normal.

Fatty tissue makes up most of the inside of the breast, which is laced with milk-producing glands (mammary glands) with ducts to the nipple. Connective tissue anchors the breasts to the pectoral muscles of the chest wall.

Before we leave the subject of breasts, let's talk about two related topics: breast self-exams and optimal breast health.

Breast Self-Examination (BSE)

In addition to a mammography (a chest X ray that women over forty should get once a year) and a breast exam conducted by your doctor (which your doctor or gynecologist should do once a year), the American Cancer Society also recommends breast self-exams (BSE) as an important tool in early cancer detection. It is true that young people rarely get breast cancer, but it is very dangerous to be lulled into a sense of complacency.

Anyone can get breast cancer, even teenagers, so it is important to know how to detect the warning signs as early as possible. If you get in the habit of BSE during the teen years, you'll be ready to continue this practice when it counts the most. By performing the exam regularly, you will become familiar with how your breasts normally feel and therefore be able to spot any irregularities quickly and early. Detecting breast cancer as early as possible greatly improves a woman's chances for successful treatment.

Since your breasts will often become tender, lumpy, or swollen just before and during your period, the best time to do a BSE is about a week after your period ends. Start the exam by standing in front of a mirror so you can see the entire surface area of each breast clearly. Look for changes in the shape of your breasts. Clasp your hands behind your head so that your breasts are raised a bit. Check for any recent changes in shape. Then put your hands on your hips and again look for changes. Study each breast carefully, looking for the following:

- **Asymmetry.** Any new asymmetry in your breasts (when one breast is a different size or shape than the other) may be an early sign of trouble. Many women have asymmetrical breasts, but if this is a new development discuss it with your doctor. A breast can become smaller if cancerous tissue is pulling in the skin.

- **Puckered or indented skin.** Puckering of the skin on the breast may indicate the presence of cancer in the connective tissue surrounding the breast ducts. Cancer growing close to the surface of the skin can also create puckering.

- **Dimpled skin.** If a lot of little dimples appear on your skin (so that it resembles the skin of an orange), speak to your doctor immediately. Dimpling can indicate the presence of a tumor that is blocking the lymph system and causing a fluid buildup.

- **Redness of the skin.** Redness of the skin of the breast is common and may indicate a simple infection. Inflammatory breast cancer, however, a rare form of breast cancer, is often characterized by redness and heat. If redness and dimpling occur simultaneously, or if redness persists, see your doctor immediately.

- **Eroded skin.** Skin that is thinning and peeling is another warning sign of cancer. Consult your doctor immediately if you notice this.

- **Retraction of the nipple.** Cancerous breast tissue may pull your nipple inward. If your nipple begins to retract in this way, see your doctor.

Examining your breasts while you are in a standing position allows you to check the upper and outer parts of your breasts where about half of breast cancers are found. Many women perform self-examinations when in the shower; breast lumps, changes, and irregularities can often be felt more easily when the skin is wet and soapy. Begin by raising your left hand and placing it behind your head. With the

The Female Body

pads of the three middle fingers of your right hand, feel for lumps in your left breast. Press firmly so that you can feel the breast tissue that lies deep below the surface of the skin. When checking the right breast, place your right hand behind your head and repeat the process with your left hand.

There are three different patterns of motion you can use to examine your breasts.

- Starting at the outer edge of the breast, near the armpit, move your fingers from the top of the breast area down to the bottom, pressing as you go and checking for lumps. Once you reach the bottom, move your fingers a little more toward the center of your breast, and go back up to the top of the breast area. Keep moving your fingers in these vertical lines up and down your breast until you reach its inner edge, near the breastbone.

- Begin at the outer edge of the breast and move around the breast, pressing with your fingers and checking for lumps, until you make a full circle. Then move your fingers a little farther toward the center of the breast and make a smaller circle. Continue with these concentric circles until you reach the nipple.

- Begin at the outer edge of the breast and move your fingers in a line extending directly toward your nipple and back. When your fingers return to their starting place, move them over a bit on the breast's outer edge and move in a straight line toward the nipple and back again. Repeat until you have made a full circle and have examined the entire breast.

Coping with PMS (Premenstrual Syndrome)

Which pattern of motion you choose is not important. What is important is that you examine the entire breast, including the underarm and upper-chest areas.

The breast self-exam should be repeated while you are lying in a reclining position. Lie down on a bed or the floor with a pillow or towel under your right shoulder and place your right arm behind your head. Check your right breast for lumps, changes, and irregularities using your preferred pattern of motion, just as you did when standing. To check your left breast, move the pillow or towel under your left shoulder, place your left arm behind your head, and repeat.

Eighty percent of breast lumps are harmless, but all lumps and other changes in the breast should be checked by a doctor. One common type of lump found in breast tissue is a cyst. Cysts are fluid-filled, partly movable sacs that seem to enlarge from water retention near the end of a period. They often disappear when the period is over. In addition to cysts, some young women have benign (harmless) movable lumps called fibroadenomas or adenofibromas.

All this may sound complicated, but with practice, examining your breasts will become easier, and it should take only ten minutes a month to perform. If you have any further questions or doubts about doing the self-examination, you can always ask your doctor. Remember, any woman can get breast cancer, even if she is in her teens. Breast cancer is still the number-two cause of cancer deaths in women, so breast self-examinations need to be taken seriously. Unfortunately, though 90 percent of breast lumps are found during BSEs, only about one-third of women regularly perform these exams. Early detection is a crucial factor in survival; 90 percent of early breast cancer is curable. That's why if you feel an unusual lump that's not going

The Female Body

away, or if you detect any other changes that seem abnormal, it's a good idea to see a doctor. Don't worry too much about not doing the self-examination right. The most important thing is to do it!

Optimal Breast Health
Not long ago, *Prevention* magazine reported on healthy breasts. The report stated that healthy breasts may have connections to a healthy diet and lifestyle. For example, breast cancer rates are four to seven times higher in the United States than in Asia. But when Asian women move to the United States, their breast-cancer risk doubles in ten years and eventually reaches United States rates. Why?

Perhaps we can link these differences to changes in diet and lifestyle. Diets for healthy breasts have much in common with eating habits that help fight PMS. We will discuss some of these healthy ways of eating in detail later on, but they include plenty of fruits and vegetables, whole-grain products, and olive oil in place of other oils. Decreasing all fats to around 30 percent of daily calories may also help. Some experts believe that giving up smoking and beverages containing caffeine also contributes to breast health.

A Woman's External Genitals

The external pelvic organs of both males and females are called genitals. Genitals are also often called reproductive organs because they make conception, pregnancy, and birth possible. If you hold a mirror between your legs, you can see the outer genitals. The vulva is another term for this entire area, which protects the opening to your urethra, your vagina, and your internal reproductive organs. The

Coping with PMS (Premenstrual Syndrome)

fleshy mound at the top of your legs, covered with hair in grown women, is call the mons or the mons pubis. The mons covers the pubic bone; the area in the middle where these bones join is called the pubic symphysis.

Before we go any further, it is important to note that women have three openings between their legs. From front to back these openings are the urethra or urinary opening, the vagina, which is the pathway for menstrual blood and through which the baby emerges during birth, and the anus, the opening for waste products to leave the body from the rectum and intestines.

The outer lips (labia majora) are two folds of skin on each side of the narrow opening to the vagina. When you reach puberty, these folds grow hair and become fuller and closer together. The inner lips (labia minor) are two smaller, hairless folds of fatty tissue that lie just inside the outer lips. Like the outer lips, the inner lips also grow during puberty and become very sensitive. The point where the top of the inner lips meet is called the clitoris. Though the part of the clitoris you can see is only about the size of a pea, it contains a large number of very sensitive nerve endings.

These nerve endings make the vestibule area (the clitoris and its shaft and linking blood vessels, tissues, and ligaments) a woman's most sensitive area. This is important for two reasons. First, before a menstrual period, this area may feel engorged (full). Second, during intercourse (sexual relations between partners) or masturbation (self-stimulation), this area becomes stimulated and can lead to orgasm, the feeling sometimes called "climax" or "coming." Not everyone masturbates, but some believe the release of tension following masturbation relieves premenstrual syndrome and the cramps that sometimes accompany menstruation and PMS.

The Female Body

The opening to the urethra (the tube that carries urine from the bladder out of the body) is right below the clitoris and above the opening to the vagina. The perineum is the area between the vagina and the anus. During childbirth, the perineum allows the relatively small, but elastic, vaginal opening to stretch in order to safely accommodate the baby's exit.

One more part of your anatomy, which you may or may not be able to see with your hand mirror, is the hymen. It is a thin, protective, and elastic strip of skin that partially covers the vaginal opening. Every young woman's hymen is different, and not everyone has one. They come in many shapes and sizes. The hymen can be torn easily, by a variety of different activities, such as sports or your first sexual intercourse. It was once thought that a broken hymen indicated that a woman must have had sex and was no longer a virgin. This is not the case. Even something like running can break your hymen. Until you have had sexual intercourse, you are a virgin, regardless of whether your hymen is intact or not.

Internal Organs

The inside gynecologic organs are the vagina, the uterus, the fallopian tubes, and the ovaries. If you have used a tampon, you know where your vagina is. Although your mirror will not reveal your inside organs, you can (with a clean finger) feel some of them.

The vagina is usually from three to five inches long. It is an elastic, muscular canal that runs from its opening below the mons pubis to your uterus. It serves as the passageway from your external genitals to your internal reproductive organs. The vaginal walls, normally collapsed on themselves like an upside-down, deflated balloon, will stretch to accommodate

Coping with PMS (Premenstrual Syndrome)

a tampon, a penis, or even a baby during birth. Menstrual blood comes from the uterus and exits through the vagina. Semen released from a man's penis will travel up the vagina, through the cervix, into the uterus, and then up into one of the fallopian tubes. If you become pregnant and give birth, the baby will travel down from the uterus and out through the vagina.

If you reach in far enough, as a doctor does when doing a pelvic exam, you might feel a hard bump at the end of the vagina. This bump is the cervix, or the bottom part of the uterus, also called the womb. It protects the inside of the uterus and provides an opening between the uterus and the vagina. The opening to the uterus in the middle of the cervix is called the os. This opening allows sperm into the uterus and menstrual blood out. This tiny opening expands greatly during childbirth to allow the baby to pass into the vagina.

The uterus is only about 2.5 inches long and is shaped like an upside-down pear. In someone who is pregnant, the uterus stretches greatly to hold the baby. It is located between the bladder and the rectum. The main purpose of the uterus is to hold and nourish a growing fetus when you are pregnant. After an egg is released by your ovary, the lining of your uterus will thicken just in case the egg becomes fertilized and an embryo begins to develop. This lining will nourish the fetus. If the egg is not fertilized, blood (and sometimes blood clots) from this disintegrated lining will pass through the cervix and out of your body through the vagina. This is your menstrual flow, or period. Though the uterus is only about the size of a fist, its walls are very muscular and elastic and have no trouble stretching to hold a fetus comfortably as it grows. The upper part of the uterus is called the fundus.

The Female Body

Extending out from each side of the fundus, like small arms with fingers at each end, are the two fallopian tubes (also called oviducts or egg ducts). The tubes are each about four to five inches long and lead to the ovaries (but are not attached to them). The unattached ends of the tube hover near the ovaries. One of the tube's fringed tips sweeps up the egg that the ovary releases and draws it into the fallopian tube. Once the egg is in the tube, it proceeds on its way to the uterus. If the egg meets a sperm while in the fallopian tube, it may become fertilized. When the fertilized egg reaches the uterus, an embryo will begin to develop.

The ovaries are located below the fallopian tubes and flank the uterus. They are round and almond-sized and are held in place by connective tissue. Though small, they contain hundreds of thousands of eggs. The eggs don't appear in the ovaries at puberty; you are born with all the eggs you will ever have. Beginning with your first menstrual cycle, one egg will ripen each month. Once ripe, it is ready to be released by the ovary. Between your first period and the onset of menopause, your ovaries will release only a small fraction of all the eggs you possess (fewer than a thousand). The ovaries also produce the female hormones estrogen and progesterone. Knowing about the work of the ovaries and the uterus in your monthly cycle is important in understanding PMS. The hormones that are produced by the ovaries play a large role in what you feel during your menstrual cycle. Now that you are aware of your special female parts, it is time to move on to ovulation and menstruation.

Ovulation and Menstruation

Before we talk about PMS, it is a good idea to know exactly what happens in your body when you get your period.

How Does Menstruation Start?

When discussing female sex hormones in chapter 1, we sketched out the process that sets your menstrual period into motion. Let's take a closer, more detailed look at that process now.

Sometime during puberty, the pituitary gland begins to send out special hormones that travel through the bloodstream to your ovaries. Hormones act as messengers that initiate actions, such as growth, elsewhere in your body. One of these hormones, the follicle-stimulating hormone (FSH), goes through your bloodstream to the ovaries. As you learned before, the ovaries contain thousands of reproductive eggs. FSH sends signals to the eggs in the ovaries to produce estrogen. Next, the increased amount of estrogen in the bloodstream signals your pituitary gland to slow down its production of FSH, which in turn tells the pituitary to make luteinizing hormone (LH). LH causes ovulation—when the ovary releases an egg. The egg then travels down one of the two fallopian tubes. Experts tell us that the ovaries alternate each month in producing a ripe egg.

Ovulation and Menstruation

Muscles in the fallopian tube contract to help the egg move toward the uterus. You may be one of the young women who actually feels ovulation as a cramp in the lower left or lower right side of your abdomen. Just before ovulation, the ovaries release progesterone. Progesterone tells your uterus to get ready for the possible arrival of a fertilized egg.

If sperm from a male has met the egg and fertilized it in the fallopian tube, the egg will implant itself in the soft, cushy endometrium (inside lining of the uterus). While estrogen causes the lining inside your uterus to grow, progesterone causes the endometrium to produce embryo-nourishing substances, which will allow a fertilized egg to develop.

If a sperm has not fertilized the egg, the egg falls apart when it enters the uterus and flows out of your body before menstruation. The production of progesterone then stops and the uterus sheds its lining. This is your menstrual period (menstruation), which in most women lasts from a few days to a week. The production of hormones slows down until your brain signals the pituitary gland to start the process all over again.

For most women, the menstrual cycle takes about twenty-eight days, but it can vary from twenty-one to forty days. Most young women get their first period between the ages of eleven and fourteen, though it can also occur as young as eight or as old as seventeen. This entire range is normal. If you are sixteen, however, and haven't gotten your first period yet, see a doctor. You may have a hormonal imbalance, which can be corrected. In general, your period will probably begin about two years after your breasts begin to develop. A woman will continue to get her period, except during pregnancy or in the case of a medical condition, until she is in her late forties, although it varies. A woman stops

Coping with PMS (Premenstrual Syndrome)

menstruating when her body doesn't produce enough estrogen to build up the uterus lining. This is called menopause.

When a girl first begins to menstruate, the cycle may not be regular. This means that you may or may not have your period at the same time every month, and it may even skip months. In the first few years of menstruation, you might get more than one period a month or no period at all for a few months. In some cases, a woman may never get on a regular, predictable cycle. But chances are you will begin to follow a regular schedule after a few months or a year. This irregular pattern can cause some problems because your period can come when you least expect it. One way to deal with this is to carry pads or tampons with you all the time. You should begin to do this as soon as your body begins to change so that when your first period comes, you will be prepared.

Your First Period and Protection

A group of young women interviewed made these comments about their first periods:

"I was scared because I didn't know what was happening."

"I wanted to get my period. My friends and I thought it would be cool."

"I was in the sixth grade, and we were studying about the monthly cycle in health class. One day, I went home and had mine. At first I was shocked—I guess I didn't think it would happen so soon. But I think it's all about becoming a woman."

"It was just a hassle."

"I was in fifth grade and felt very uncomfortable because I was one of the first of my group of friends to get it."

Ovulation and Menstruation

"It's a part of life—no big deal."

When young women first start having periods, many use pads, which are technically called sanitary napkins. Pads are made of paper and other absorbent fibers. Pads have adhesive strips that you attach directly to your underwear. They have a fluid-proof shield inside that protects against leaking and staining. Pads come in many sizes and shapes. Some are thick to protect against a heavy flow. These are called maxipads by the companies that make them. Some pads are very thin and can be used toward the end of your period or when you think you might get your period. These are called minipads or panty shields. You may want to try different shapes and sizes of pads until you find the one that suits your needs.

Eventually you may decide to try internal protection, or tampons. Most tampons have an applicator that makes the tampon easy to insert and a string that makes it easy to pull out. Tampons take some getting used to, but once you learn how to insert them, you may decide to stop wearing pads, or wear them only at night. Many women find tampons more comfortable to wear because they don't feel them. For starters, get the smallest (thinnest) tampon you can find; a junior size might be just right. Tampons come in a variety of sizes. Some tampons are deodorized or scented. It's better to use the unscented kind to prevent any allergic reaction. Once your body adjusts to using tampons, you can start using larger, more absorbent ones if you need them. A more absorbent tampon can accommodate more blood flow. Some women need a super-absorbent tampon for the first few days, and then switch to a less-absorbent "regular" or "junior" tampon.

Coping with PMS (Premenstrual Syndrome)

Remove the outer wrapper of the tampon. Then read the directions that come in the box. These instructions are very important, so be sure to follow them carefully. The toilet seat is a good place to sit while inserting a tampon because the vaginal walls angle toward the back of your body; they don't go straight up. However, some young women prefer to stand up or lie down when inserting a tampon. It is all a matter of personal preference.

If the tampon is inserted properly, you should not feel it at all. Learning how to insert a tampon can take some time. It can be frustrating, especially if you are unfamiliar with your anatomy. Some women use a mirror to help them see better the first time they insert a tampon. After you get the hang of it, though, you'll be able to do it with ease. It also helps to use tampons that are the correct absorbency. If a tampon is hard to take out when it is time to change it, try a less absorbent tampon.

An important thing to remember about tampons is that you must change them often, at least three times a day, every six to eight hours. A very serious condition called toxic shock syndrome (TSS) can be caused by not changing tampons frequently enough. TSS is caused by a variation of the bacteria *Staphylococcus aureus*, which in rare cases secretes a potent toxin. It is a rare disease, but it can be deadly. Its symptoms include vomiting, diarrhea, dizziness and fainting, weakness, aching muscles and joints, fever, red eyes, sore throat, and a rash. Your chances of getting TSS increase if you use tampons, especially if you don't change them frequently. Research conducted by the Centers for Disease Control indicates that the more absorbent the tampon, the higher the risk of TSS. This is because high-absorbency tampons can cause vaginal dryness and chafing

Ovulation and Menstruation

of the vaginal wall; broken skin increases your risk of contracting the disease. As a result, women are often cautioned against using high-absorbency tampons.

If you notice any TSS symptoms and you are wearing a tampon, remove it immediately and do not insert a new one. Call your doctor right away. If diagnosed early, TSS can be treated successfully with antibiotics and intravenous fluids. You should feel perfectly safe, however, using tampons as long as you follow the package directions for insertion, removal, and regular changing.

Keep in mind that TSS is a rare disease; less than one-fifth of one percent of menstruating women ever get it. In addition, the number of TSS cases has decreased dramatically in the past twenty years. In 1980, 814 cases of TSS were reported, compared with only 5 confirmed cases in 1997.

Many misconceptions exist about the link between tampons and TSS. Recently, many false rumors have been circulating widely on the Internet concerning the supposed dangers of tampons. Some of these suggest that U.S. tampon manufacturers add asbestos to tampons to increase menstrual bleeding in order to boost sales of tampons. The Food and Drug Administration (FDA) reviews the design and the materials of all tampons sold in the United States; it reports that asbestos is not an ingredient in any U.S.-made brand of tampon. Other rumors suggest that some tampons contain toxic amounts of the chemical dioxin. Tampons sold in the United States are made of cotton or rayon or a blend of the two. Rayon is made from fibers derived from wood pulp. At one time this pulp was bleached with chlorine to make it white, and this chlorine did indeed contain small amounts of dioxin. Today, however, the bleaching process is chlorine-free, and dioxin levels in rayon are undetectable.

Six Ways to Relieve Cramps

1. **Over-the-counter painkillers.** A general painkiller, such as ibuprofen, or one specifically designed for period cramps, such as Midol, may help relieve your pain. A word of caution: Don't take any drug, even a nonprescription drug, without asking your doctor about it first. Any drug can be harmful. You may be allergic to it or it may react poorly with other medication you are taking. It is best to get advice from your doctor in advance and read the instructions and warning notices on the package carefully.

2. **Apply heat.** Warmth helps loosen tight and cramped muscles. It can also be very soothing. Take a long, hot bath or place a heating pad on your abdomen.

3. **Exercise.** Exercise causes the release of the brain's "feel good" chemicals that act as natural painkillers and mood enhancers. Exercise also helps loosen up your muscles. When your muscles are relaxed, stress and pain are relieved.

4. **Diet.** Although you may be craving salty food during your period, you should cut back on salt. By eating less salt and drinking more water, you flush out your system and reduce bloating and cramps. Avoiding caffeine and alcohol also seems to help relieve many women of their cramping and bloating.

5. **Massage.** Gentle rubbing or massaging of your abdomen can also help relieve your cramps.

6. **Sleep.** Make sure you get enough sleep. Being tired and in pain makes it much harder to cope.

Ovulation and Menstruation

Whatever you decide to use when you have your period, remember to change the product frequently. This is important for your health and will make you feel cleaner.

Cramps

Sometimes you might feel discomfort or cramps right before or during the first day or two of your period. This is normal. The cramps are caused by contractions of the uterine muscles. These contractions are your body's way of trying to release and absorb prostaglandin, a hormone-like chemical that is activated right before the beginning of your period.

Some women get severe cramps that do not go away. If this happens, see a doctor as soon as possible. He or she will be able to help you deal with the pain. As we said before, your period will usually last anywhere from three to seven days. Some days, your flow will be heavier than others, but if it is heavy for more than one week, you need to go to the doctor. If you bleed between periods, you should tell the doctor. Overall, understanding what a normal menstrual cycle is like will help you manage your period.

Now that you know all about the normal menstrual cycle, let's see what happens in women who have PMS.

PMS

The study of premenstrual symptoms has a long history, possibly beginning with Hippocrates (460–377 BC), the father of modern medicine. Only recently, however, have researchers taken PMS seriously enough to conduct scientific studies on various treatments.

According to various sources, in 1931, R. T. Frank, an American neurologist, first used the term "premenstrual tension" to describe symptoms occurring in the luteal phase (just after ovulation) of the menstrual cycle. Yet most doctors continued to think of their patients' premenstrual symptoms as being "all in their heads." Because women were viewed as the "weaker sex," PMS was considered to be a kind of hysteria and was therefore treated with antidepressants and sedatives. In 1953, however, Dr. Katharina Dalton from Great Britain, a pioneer in the treatment of PMS, popularized the term "premenstrual syndrome." This term characterized the symptoms as having a hormonal (rather than an emotional) basis, and Dalton advocated treating the physical symptoms—through the use of progesterone suppositories—rather than numbing the patients' minds.

What Is PMS?

Premenstrual syndrome refers to more than 150 symptoms (emotional, physical, and behavioral) that occur consistently in successive menstrual cycles. They appear in the days before your period begins and disrupt normal functioning. They improve during the menstrual period, and they go away after menstruation has stopped. PMS usually occurs a week or ten days before the start of a menstrual period, in the luteal phase of the menstrual cycle. In other words, the beginning of a menstrual period usually relieves the symptoms of PMS. One expert put it this way: "If you don't have a couple of weeks free of symptoms after your period starts, you don't have PMS." Some women insist that their premenstrual syndrome continues for one to three days into the period, and some even say they have symptoms until menstruation stops. Other women say they experience PMS all month and their symptoms just get more intense before their period. A few women report having both PMS and dysmenorrhea (painful menstruation).

This book, however, will define PMS as symptoms that occur seven to ten days before the menstrual period starts. By our definition, you should have some problem-free, good days after the first day of your period. Also, by this definition, PMS should occur for several cycles and be severe enough to disrupt your life in some way, such as forcing you to take days off from work or school; causing emotional outbursts directed at family, friends, and coworkers; creating obsessive cravings for food or alcohol; or giving you uncontrollable crying spells and depression.

Recognizing Symptoms

The list on page 29 contains the most common PMS symptoms. The physical ones are on the left and the emotional or psychological ones are on the right. It's vital to notice the pattern of your symptoms; when they occur is more important than what they are. You will not have the exact same symptoms every month, and they will not always last for the same amount of time or be of the same intensity.

What Causes It?

Scientists have been unable to determine any one cause of PMS, even though they have been trying to do so for more than fifty years. The theories range widely, with most arguing for a hormonal, chemical, nutritional, and psychological basis for PMS. It seems likely that PMS is caused by some combination of all of these.

Hormones

Some women may experience a greater shift in hormone levels (particularly estrogen and progesterone) before their periods, or they may simply be more sensitive than other women are to normal monthly hormone shifts. Hormones released during the menstrual cycle, such as prolactin, may cause unpleasant physical and emotional effects, such as breast tenderness and mood swings. Prolactin may also be the culprit in a menstrual disorder known as amenorrhea—irregular, infrequent, or discontinued periods. Excessive production of aldosterone and other mineral corticoids (hormones that regulate the body's processing of fluids and electrolytes, such as sodium and potassium)

Physical

Abdominal cramps
Acne (pimples and other skin disorders)
Allergies
Backaches
Bloating (water retention and swelling of body tissues)
Bodyaches
Breast swelling and tenderness
Clumsiness
Constipation
Decreased coordination
Diarrhea
Dizziness
Fatigue
Headaches
Heart palpitations
Hot flashes
Increased appetite or thirst
Infections
Insomnia (inability to sleep)
Joint pain
Muscle spasms
Muscle stiffness
Nausea
Numbness, prickling, tingling, or sensitivity of arms and/or legs
Pelvic pressure
Skin inflammation and itchiness
Sweating
Weight gain

Emotional/Psychological

Agitation
Anger
Anxiety
Concentration problems
Confusion
Crying spells
Decreased self-esteem
Depression
Emotional hypersensitivity
Forgetfulness
Hostility
Insomnia or other sleep disturbances
Irritability
Loneliness
Loss of self-control
Mood swings
Nervousness
Nightmares
Paranoia (the feeling that someone is out to get you)
Restlessness
Suicidal thoughts
Tension

may cause bloating, as can temporary sodium and water retention by the kidneys. Some researchers think PMS sufferers may be overly sensitive to progesterone.

Neurochemicals
Low levels of serotonin and gamma-aminobutyric acid, chemicals that send neurological messages from one cell to the next, have been linked with depression and anxiety, and some researchers feel they may play a part in PMS, too. A similar lack of endorphins—the body's natural painkilling and mood-enhancing neurochemicals—may also play a role in the acute discomfort and moodiness associated with PMS.

Nutrition
Many women report experiencing more mild PMS symptoms after they make dietary changes, such as avoiding salty and fatty foods, alcohol, and caffeine, and increasing their intake of calcium-rich foods and complex carbohydrates (such as potatoes, rice, bread, pasta, fruits, and vegetables). Sometimes PMS sufferers also have hypoglycemia (low blood sugar, a condition that can make you feel fatigued and faint). Some researchers believe there may be a link between low blood sugar and PMS.

Depression
Though PMS is now generally recognized as a primarily physical disorder, its many mood-related symptoms have led some scientists to speculate on possible psychological causes. Roughly 60 percent of women who suffer from depression or other mood disorders have also been diagnosed with PMS. It is estimated that between 60 and 100

PMS Symptom Groups

In the early 1980s, medical researcher Guy Abraham, M.D., classified the symptoms of PMS into four main categories:

A Anxiety, irritability, crying spells, feeling out of control. This is the most common PMS category; some 80 percent of women have experienced these PMS symptoms.

C Cravings for sweets, chocolate, salty foods, dairy products, and alcohol. Almost one out of four women with PMS report carbohydrate cravings. The initial spike and resulting crash in blood sugar levels following the consumption of sweets can cause PMS-like symptoms, such as irritability and fatigue.

D Depression, confusion, clumsiness, forgetfulness, fear, paranoia, suicidal thoughts.

H Heaviness, headache, bloating, breast tenderness, and weight gain caused by fluid retention. This is the second most common group of PMS symptoms, experienced by 60 percent of women.

In recent years, some doctors have added a fifth category of PMS symptoms: category P. This group of symptoms relates to an increased sensitivity to pain. This pain usually takes the form of cramps and aches in the back, the head, and the joints.

percent of women diagnosed with PMS have also experienced at least one period of depression, compared to no more than 20 percent of women who do not suffer from PMS. Even if there is a link between depression and PMS, however, PMS is not "all in your head." Depression can often be due to chemical imbalances rather than emotional or psychological problems. This may be the case with PMS.

Genetics

There may also be a genetic link to PMS. Some studies have shown that if your mother or sisters suffer from PMS, you are more likely to experience its symptoms, too.

What Cures It?

No one has found a specific cure for this frustrating condition. In the past, because there was no specific cause and no specific cure, some people refused to admit that PMS existed. Even today there are those with doubts about PMS. Those doubters are at one end of a range of beliefs about this condition. At the other end of the range are those who blame everything that goes wrong or any extreme emotional state on PMS. Somewhere in the middle are those who recognize PMS as a cluster of symptoms, each of which needs individual treatment. More recently, researchers have begun to take a serious look at the possible causes of PMS and have intensified their efforts to cure it. Although there is no simple cure, there are treatments that provide relief for the painful symptoms of PMS. These will be discussed in detail later in the book.

Does Everyone Get PMS?

As many as 75 to 80 percent of women experience some PMS symptoms during their reproductive years. These can include emotional sensitivity, crying episodes, irritability, tension, and moodiness. Cravings for sweet or salty foods are experienced by 75 percent of women. Some women have hot flashes, heart palpitations, dizziness, and upset stomachs. For most women, these symptoms tend to be mild and do not require treatment. Their intensity varies from woman to woman and may last anywhere from a few hours to several days. However, 30 to 40 percent of women experience symptoms that are severe enough to disrupt their daily lives. Somewhere between 3 and 8 percent of women have symptoms so extreme that they are disabled by the condition, which is referred to as premenstrual dysphoric disorder.

PMS can occur at any time in your life after puberty. If you have it as a teenager, it doesn't mean that you'll always have it. On the other hand, if you don't have PMS as a teen, it doesn't mean that you'll never get it. The majority of teens do not get PMS; but for those who do, the symptoms can be rough. Adolescent girls with PMS may suffer more than older women, says Marla Ahlgrimm, founder and president of the Women's Health America Group in Madison, Wisconsin.

PMS Is Not All Bad

People tend to think of PMS as negative, but some women report a few positive symptoms, such as increased energy, more creativity, and a greater ability to accomplish various tasks.

Recording: Making Your PMS Chart

Now that you've recognized some possible PMS symptoms, do your "charting." Charting will accomplish several goals. First, it will help you remember your symptoms from one month to the next, even from one year to the next. Second, it will help you and any medical experts you consult to figure out if the symptoms are clustered in the time frame we discussed—before your period, in the luteal phase of your cycle. If your symptoms do not cluster in the luteal phase, it doesn't mean you don't have PMS; it may mean you have additional problems. Third, charting or recordkeeping will help you zero in on which symptoms are troublesome enough to require treatment. You can see an example of a PMS chart on page 35.

Charting may sound complicated, but it isn't. Perhaps you can do it before you go to bed each night. Try to write something about your thoughts and feelings every day. That way you'll get into the habit of recordkeeping. Also, if you write something on the good days, you will have a combination of positive and negative thoughts, which will help put things into perspective on those bad days. You can make your chart elaborate if you want to; you can even use illustrations. But you can also keep it as simple as writing everything in a journal. Recognizing when and what your symptoms are will help you stay in control of your life. Nothing is more frustrating than feeling angry or depressed and having no real reason for those feelings. Often it's a relief to say, "I'm not crazy. It's PMS that's making me feel this way." It is easy to forget about how PMS can make you feel, even if you get it every month.

My PMS Chart

January	February	March
1		
2		
3		
4		
5		
6		
7		
8		
9		
10		
11		
12		
13		
14		
15		
16		
17		
18		
19		
20		
21		
22		
23		
24		
25		
26		
27		
28		
29		
30		
31		

Coping with PMS (Premenstrual Syndrome)

Becca says, "It was the funniest thing. PMS was driving me crazy. Every month for a couple of days before my period, I had headaches, backaches, or felt sick to my stomach. I faithfully wrote everything in my journal. A few months ago when I went back and read what I'd written, I realized how happy I was to get my period. I decided I could put up with PMS because I knew it would end in a few days."

Some people keep a notebook for their chart. You can also use a daily or a weekly calendar, or even a diary if you prefer. Or you can make up a chart on a computer. Make three columns. Head the columns with the first three months of your record. Then, in the left margin, make rows for each day of the month up to thirty-one.

Write down the date when each menstrual period begins. Include on your chart any medications you are taking and the dosage (amount). Some health professionals suggest writing down the severity (intensity) of your symptoms or rating them with a number: 1=mild, 2=medium, 3=severe. Or, if you prefer, you can write something like "bad cramps" or "mild headache."

You do not have to have a certain number of symptoms to have PMS. Some women have more physical symptoms, others have more emotional difficulties. Jill has some of each. "I crave sweets. I eat a lot. I feel bloated and lack energy. My mood goes from top-of-the-world to down-in-the-dumps in a matter of minutes." Some young women have only one PMS symptom every month. Some have different problems each month. If you have any of these symptoms, you can ignore them or put up with them as Becca did. Or you may be ready to do something about them.

PMS

Allison is a person who decided to do something. She says, "Every month about a week before my period, I got a craving for french fries with gravy. I'm trying to eat healthy foods, and I didn't want to give in to my craving. Every month I wrote down how I felt. I realized I couldn't stop thinking about fries. Finally, I decided to give my body what it wanted. Once I had what I wanted, I felt satisfied and stopped craving them. It felt good to take control and get some relief. The longer I denied myself, the worse I felt. PMS is hard enough to handle. Why should I beat myself up over an order of fries?"

What PMS Is Not

PMS is a series of symptoms that are sometimes hard to pin down. Those who don't pay attention to the special characteristics and timing of premenstrual syndrome may confuse it with any number of other conditions. Other conditions may have PMS-like symptoms, but there are important differences. Often, our understanding of something as intangible as PMS increases by learning what it is not. Here are some different conditions that could be confused with PMS.

Dysmenorrhea (Painful Menstruation)
In Greek, *dys* means "difficult," *men* means "month," and *rhoia* means "flow." So there we have the definition: a difficult monthly flow. Unlike PMS, dysmenorrhea occurs at the beginning of the menstrual period and during it. The most prominent symptom is cramping or pain in the lower abdomen and pelvic area.

Coping with PMS (Premenstrual Syndrome)

Cramps are a part of most women's menstrual cycles. Ten percent, however, suffer from dysmenorrhea, which is a more severe form of cramps and which usually starts a year or two after a girl starts having her period. The cramps may get worse until a young woman is about twenty years old; then dysmenorrhea tends to lessen. Recent research blames hormones called prostaglandins for causing uterine contractions, as well as backaches, headaches, nausea, and vomiting in some people.

Although dysmenorrhea is not a serious health hazard, it can be a pain, causing some people to miss school or work. Some treatments used for PMS also help dysmenorrhea.

Endometriosis

Endometriosis occurs when pieces of the endometrium (lining of the uterus) break off, escape from the uterus, and become implanted on other organs, such as the ovaries, the fallopian tubes, and the uterus. The endometrial cells mimic the menstrual cycle by thickening and bleeding, but because the cells are attached to other organs, the blood has nowhere to go.

Endometriosis can cause pain, sometimes before a menstrual period and on into the period. The stray cells eventually form blisters, scars, and sometimes adhesions (abnormal scar tissue that holds organs together). These scars and adhesions can prevent pregnancy. Experts used to say that endometriosis did not begin until a woman's late twenties or early thirties. Newer studies show that more than half of women with endometriosis experienced symptoms before the age of twenty-five. Most times, endometriosis doesn't need treatment. But occasionally it progresses and becomes more painful. To diagnose it properly, a doctor will use a laparoscope, a slim instrument inserted into the abdomen. It has a light on the end and allows a doctor to examine your pelvic organs. Birth control pills are used to treat the symptoms. Surgery may be needed, however, if the pill doesn't work.

Pelvic Inflammatory Disease (PID)

Pelvic inflammatory disease (PID) is an infection that is sometimes, but not always, the result of sexual activity. If it is the result of sexual activity, it is called a sexually transmitted disease (STD). Originally the term PID described inflammation of the fallopian tubes; now it is used to describe infections of any of the reproductive organs of the pelvis.

In the acute or early phase, the pain of PID can be severe; in the chronic or later phase, the pain may be more like the discomfort of dysmenorrhea or PMS—lower abdominal aches and backaches. In either situation, consult a doctor. An unpleasant-smelling discharge may accompany PID, along with other symptoms, such as chills, fever, and urinary problems. Doctors usually treat PID with antibiotics (often both for the woman and her sexual partner) and pain-relieving medications.

Pelvic Pain Syndrome

It is also possible for some women to experience considerable pelvic pain about seven to ten days before menstruation. In addition to pain when sitting or standing, a young woman may feel symptoms similar to PMS, such as insomnia or headaches. If you are experiencing pelvic pain, speak to your doctor about it.

Coping with PMS (Premenstrual Syndrome)

Depression
Although PMS may make you feel depressed, you should have some days after your period starts during which you feel happy (or at least not sad). Depression is an overwhelmingly sad feeling that does not go away—not even when good things happen or when a menstrual period starts. Major depression is serious: Nine million Americans suffer from it, and in the most severe cases the possibility of suicide is a concern. The following are common symptoms of depression: loss of interest in formerly pleasurable activities, loss of energy, sleep disorders (sleeping too much or not being able to sleep), difficulty concentrating, feelings of despair and hopelessness, and inability to eat or eating too much. If you have some of these symptoms and they persist, don't excuse the situation as PMS; talk to a parent, a counselor, or a doctor right away.

Once you have pinpointed your PMS symptoms, the next step is to help yourself relieve the pain and the discomfort you are experiencing. Helping yourself can include a combination of lifestyle changes—from diet and exercise to relaxation techniques and counseling.

Lifestyle Changes

What is lifestyle, and why is it important in the treatment of PMS? Lifestyle refers to your diet, how much you sleep and relax, and your relationship with yourself and other people. In general, it means how you live. You can make lifestyle changes after some careful thought and a bit of research. Maybe you already have a healthy lifestyle. But you can always pick up a tip or two about becoming more healthy and further improving your chances of beating PMS.

Improving your lifestyle is important for three reasons. First, consider the connections between your mental and physical well-being and PMS. Scientists continue to explore how negative states (stress, worry, anger, and depression) affect the development of premenstrual syndrome. Positive states, such as a sense of peacefulness, a sense of humor, and an optimistic outlook, help fight the effects of PMS.

Second, medical science has not done much more than women themselves have done in treating premenstrual syndrome. Many doctors believe that the single most important thing in treating PMS is a healthy lifestyle. Simple changes, such as getting more sleep or eating more fruits and vegetables, have worked better than medicine in many cases. Further, a direct link may exist between certain dietary substances, such as caffeine, sugar, and salt, and the severity of PMS symptoms. One treatment theory recommends avoiding the quick drop in blood sugar associated with eating the processed sugar in junk food. A sudden drop in blood sugar releases adrenaline, a hormone that increases blood pressure and stimulates the heart. When adrenaline is released into the bloodstream, the progesterone receptors in the cells cannot work properly. To keep blood sugar up, eat five or six small meals a day or have frequent snacks.

Third, when you make lifestyle changes, such as exercising every day (or every other day), you are taking control of your life, which is an important step in fighting PMS. Making healthy changes will give you a feeling of empowerment, which is a valuable life skill, not just a way to combat PMS. Studies have shown that women who take charge of their lives by doing their own problem solving and handling their anger constructively are more likely than others to do well in fighting PMS.

When you make lifestyle changes, some of your friends may not be supportive. They may tease you because your changes feel threatening to them. But if you stick to what you're doing, they may end up following your lead. You will find some advice for family and friends in chapter 6.

Food and Drink: The Spices of Life

Before we discuss specific foods, it is important to acknowledge the role that food plays in our lives. For some of us, eating is a way of coping with stress. Frances says, "As a way of treating my PMS, I used to come home after school and put a couple of frozen dinners in the microwave. Then I'd carry

Lifestyle Changes

my food downstairs to the TV room. I'd stretch out sideways on the futon and shovel that food in, hardly aware of what I was doing. Afterward, I'd feel sluggish and unhappy, but I'd turn around and do the same thing the next day. Finally, after doing some reading about PMS, I asked my mom not to buy any more of those dinners. Now I go to the gym after school and work out with a friend. I feel 100 percent better."

Frances was smart to understand that she was using food in an unhealthy way to handle stress. Most of us take food for granted. But because PMS treatment is linked to good eating, it is important to learn some of those healthy habits.

One idea is to write down everything you eat for three to five days. You can make this part of your PMS journal. Try to remember how you were feeling when you ate a bag of potato chips and a candy bar. How did you feel afterward?

Part of healthy eating is staying health conscious most of the time. Once in a while if you get a craving, it is OK to indulge. Try not to let your indulgences become an unhealthy pattern. Cravings often go away once they are satisfied anyway. Those who eat well learn to do it automatically. If you are trying to start this new pattern and want to know what foods seem to work best for PMS, give your food choices some thought.

We will start with the foods you eat and the liquids you drink. Let's see what you can take out of your diet and what you can add. Both actions will have benefits. You'll find that food doesn't have to be bad for you for it to taste good. And food doesn't have to taste bad in order to be good for you. As you take out certain foods or drinks and put others in, do it one food or drink at a time, so you can tell what's working and what is not. Record this information on your PMS chart or in your journal. This way you'll remember how you felt after you ate a certain food. Observe dietary changes all month long, not just when you're "PMS-ing." With today's labeling of foods, it is easy to keep track of harmful ingredients and food additives. Just look on the back of the package to see what is inside the food you are eating. It is important to moderate your intake of salt, sugar, and caffeine to lead a healthy lifestyle.

What to Take Out

Caffeine
Caffeine, a stimulant, increases sleeplessness, anxiety, and tension, which are all parts of the PMS problem. Though caffeine can provide you with a quick pick-me-up, this is only a temporary energy boost. Once the initial, short-lived rush burns off, you will feel more tired and down than before you had caffeine. Better to take a ten-minute nap or go to bed early. "Jacking" yourself up with caffeine will ultimately disappoint you. Caffeine is also psychologically and physically addictive.

Because caffeine can have these negative effects on your mood, it is a good idea to minimize your caffeine consumption, or give it up altogether, especially in the week before your period begins. Be careful how you cut back or give it up, however. Rapid caffeine withdrawal may cause extreme sluggishness, fatigue, and headaches. To avoid these, try cutting back on caffeine slowly over time. Withdrawal symptoms are temporary and should not last more than two weeks. Like other dietary items you take out or add, give the change a chance; several months is not too long to keep trying. Remember, too, that caffeine is not only

Lifestyle Changes

found in coffee. Large amounts of caffeine are also found in tea, soft drinks, chocolate (including hot chocolate), and some over-the-counter medications.

Sugar

It is a good idea to try to remove as much sugar from your diet as possible. Sugar has many different names, including dextrose, fructose, lactose, maltose, and sucrose. If you see more than one of these names listed on a package, the food may contain more sugar than you thought. Other sugary substances, such as corn syrup, maple syrup, honey, molasses, and even sugar substitutes, imitate sugar.

Sugar is a simple carbohydrate that stimulates the pancreas to produce high levels of insulin. Insulin not only makes you hungry but also increases the triglycerides (fats) in your blood and increases the risk of heart disease. After an insulin infusion, your blood sugar levels will plummet, leaving you tired and irritable. Like caffeine, sugar picks you up, then drops you with a jolt.

Refined sugar is not easy to eliminate from your diet. It pops up in everything, including candy, condiments like ketchup, sauces like prepared spaghetti sauce, and baked goods such as bread, muffins, and cakes. Caffeine, salt, fat, and sugar all "hide" in foods. A good example is cold cereal. Check the label on the side of the box. Is sugar the first ingredient listed? If so, try a different one, perhaps one with wheat as the first ingredient. Ingredients on a package are listed in descending order by the amount included. If an ingredient such as sugar is listed first or second, beware. It means sugar is a main ingredient. In addition, many juice drinks are mostly sugar. If possible, drink real juice.

Coping with PMS (Premenstrual Syndrome)

Salt

Salt (sodium chloride) holds water in body tissues. In some women with PMS, sodium seems to contribute to bloating. If you don't have problems with bloating, you do not need to worry so much. But even health experts consider excess sodium a long-range danger because it can cause high blood pressure, which later in life can cause strokes and other health problems. Most Americans ingest 4,000 to 6,000 milligrams of salt a day. Eating a lot of processed foods, such as hot dogs and frozen pizza, can increase your daily salt intake to 10,000 milligrams. To avoid excessive fluid retention before and during your period, try to restrict your salt intake to 2,000 to 4,000 milligrams a day. Eliminating the use of table salt, eating fresh rather than processed food, reading ingredient lists carefully, and changing what you order in restaurants can help you reach this target.

In place of salt, you can use lemon juice or vinegar on vegetables and salads. Try spices on your popcorn, such as dried onion, garlic powder, or dried peppers. Many people, especially those with heart conditions, must limit their sodium intake. You can take advantage of the many products made for people on a low-sodium diet.

Fat

Nutrition experts say that fat calories should make up about 30 percent of your total food intake each day. Some doctors recommend that women who suffer from PMS try to reduce fat to 20 percent of their diet. Most Americans eat much more fat than that. Too much fat in your diet, and not enough regular exercise, can lead to heart problems.

Lifestyle Changes

Keep in mind that many high-fat foods, such as bacon, sausage, hot dogs, and hard cheeses, are also high in sodium. Other high-fat foods, such as cakes, cookies, rolls, and doughnuts, also contain a lot of sugar. They may taste good but probably won't make you feel so good if you eat too much of them. Avoid trans-fatty acids in particular (the kind of fat found in margarine and many snack foods). Trans-fatty acids raise the level of lipoprotein in your blood, increasing your risk of cardiovascular disease. Human beings need to ingest fat, but some sources of fat are better than others. Olive oil, fish, nuts, and avocados all contain the kind of fatty acid that can actually boost your "good" cholesterol and reduce your "bad" cholesterol. They contain unsaturated fats that lower lipoprotein levels, reducing your risk of heart disease. In general, cutting down on high-fat foods will help relieve your PMS symptoms. It will also give you more energy and a longer, healthier life.

Alcohol

If you're under twenty-one, it is illegal for you to drink alcohol. But people under twenty-one do sometimes drink alcohol. Using alcohol to try to alleviate your PMS symptoms can often make them worse. For one thing, alcohol, like caffeine, can negatively affect your mood. It can also restrict blood flow to your brain, causing headaches. Furthermore, alcoholic drinks contain the sugar you are trying to avoid. Some women report an increase in bloating after drinking alcohol. Because it is a potentially addictive drug and because women may be more sensitive to its effects before their periods, it is best to avoid alcohol altogether.

Excess Food

In her book *Self-Help for Premenstrual Syndrome*, Michelle Harrison, M.D., writes that the diet for PMS is not a weight-loss diet and that neither gaining nor losing weight will help. But if PMS makes you feel heavy, sluggish, and bloated, try eliminating excess food. Eat a little less than you usually do, or consider the old adage to "leave the table a little bit hungry." Try five or six small meals, or a fruit, vegetable, or high-grain snack every two or three hours to maintain a proper blood sugar level.

What to Add

Now that you have removed (or at least limited) some harmful substances from your diet, you're ready to "add in." Adding foods will be a lot more fun than taking them out, so try to concentrate on what you can eat rather than on what you cannot eat. This will help you stick with a healthy diet. (You may find the recipes at the end of the book helpful.)

Complex Carbohydrates

Complex carbohydrates include fruits, vegetables, rice, cereals, grains, pasta, and legumes (dried beans and peas). You can combine whole grains (cereals and breads) with legumes to provide a complete protein (of the kind you would get by eating meat). Most experts recommend that complex carbohydrates make up between 50 and 60 percent of your daily diet. For information on nutritious meatless meals, see *Laurel's Kitchen* by Laurel Robertson, Carol Flinders, and Bronwen Godfrey; *Diet for a Small Planet* by Frances Moore Lappe; Jane Brody's cookbooks; and many others that you can probably find in your local library.

Lifestyle Changes

In contrast to sugar (a simple carbohydrate), which provides a quick burst of energy followed by a crash, the sugars from complex carbohydrates enter the bloodstream more slowly and provide a more sustained source of energy for your body. By avoiding sudden, sharp fluctuations in your blood sugar level, you are minimizing your risk of experiencing the mood-related disturbances of PMS. Complex carbohydrates may actually provide a natural boost to your mood; they have been shown to stimulate the production of certain endorphins (the brain's natural "feel good" chemicals), resulting in improved mood and reduced tension. The abundance of vitamins and minerals in vegetables, fruits, legumes, and grains, such as iron, calcium, magnesium, manganese, the B vitamins, and vitamin E may also help relieve your PMS symptoms. Some research shows that these vitamins and minerals are effective as a natural remedy for the mood swings, bloating, cramps, bodyaches, and food cravings associated with PMS.

Vegetables

Most people today like their veggies raw, stir-fried, or steamed so they are still nice and crunchy. Some vegetables, such as broccoli, are more digestible when cooked. The less you cook vegetables the more vitamins they retain. Nutritionists recommend that you eat at least three servings of vegetables per day.

In case you are not familiar with many vegetables besides lettuce, celery, carrots, and the others already mentioned, here are a few for you to get to know: artichokes, beets, cabbage, collard greens, corn, cucumbers, eggplant, endive, kale, kohlrabi, leeks, mushrooms, okra, peppers, potatoes, pumpkin, radishes, spinach, turnips, and yams. Don't forget to experiment with different kinds of lettuce; iceberg lettuce contains lots of water but doesn't have as many vitamins as do the dark green, leafy varieties, such as romaine.

Fruits
Most people like fruit. There are many different types of fruit available, from apples, bananas, and berries to cantaloupe, grapes, kiwis, mangos, pears, papayas, and peaches—and a whole lot more! In fact, the biggest problem can be eating too much. (Fruit contains simple sugar. It is natural sugar, but it's still sugar.) One solution may be to limit your consumption to two or three pieces of fruit a day, until you see how your body reacts to it.

Fresh fruits can be very expensive, especially out of season. Everyone says "eat fruit," but few mention how much it costs. Many fruits are available dried, such as apples, cranberries, or bananas. Remind your parents or other relatives that fruit is important for the health of the whole family, and if they haven't been keeping it in the house already, they'll be sure to buy it.

Grains
These days, whole grains are in. When your mom was your age, she may not have heard of the nourishing grain couscous, a cracked-wheat product. If she had wanted some, she would have had to find a health-food store. Now you'll find couscous and other whole-grain products in any supermarket. Back then, people also liked their flour and rice to be white. But recently people learned that manufacturers were taking out the best part, the whole grain. By checking the wrapper, you can tell if bread is 100

Lifestyle Changes

percent whole wheat or whole grain. When you bake, use wheat flour instead of white flour. Whole-wheat pasta is available on most grocery shelves.

For breakfast, you can make your own hot cereal from whole grains, such as cracked wheat. It takes only a little longer to make the much more nutritious, quick-cooking oatmeal rather than the instant kind. If you have an occasional cookie, choose oatmeal raisin. Instead of white rice, use brown rice, bulghur (a kind of cracked wheat), or couscous. Corn is a crossover food because it is a vegetable that is sometimes ground into meal (cornmeal). Popcorn that is popped in just a little oil makes an excellent snack. Other grains include barley, millet, oats, rye, and triticale (a cross between wheat and rye). Grains appear in cereals, flours, breads, pastas, and as an ingredient in soups.

Legumes (Dried Beans and Peas)

You don't hear much talk about legumes, but dried beans and peas are loaded with protein, B vitamins, and iron. Soybeans, for example, produce the following useful by-products: tofu (solidly curdled soy milk), bean sprouts, soy milk, soy nuts, soy flakes, and soy grits. Other legumes are black beans, black-eyed peas, chickpeas (garbanzos), kidney beans, lentils, lima beans, mung beans, peanuts, pinto beans, split peas, and white beans.

Seeds and Nuts

Nuts are actually the "fruit" of trees. Although nuts contain a lot of fat, doctors and nutritionists point out that they are good for you. Nuts contain mono- and polyunsaturated fats, not the harmful saturated fat found in many fried foods. In addition, nuts give you fiber. An ounce of nuts contains about as much fiber as two slices of wheat bread. Nuts also contain vitamin E, which some research suggests improves heart health and increases brain power. There are many different kinds of seeds and nuts, such as almonds, Brazil nuts, cashews, chestnuts, filberts or hazelnuts, macadamia nuts, pecans, pine nuts, pistachios, pumpkin and sunflower seeds, and walnuts.

Other Treats You Can Eat
No one has said that to beat PMS you have to live on fruits, vegetables, pasta, grains, and nuts. If you like meat, you can have it once in a while. In moderation, lean meat, such as round steak, pork tenderloin, boneless ham, chicken (skinless), and fish are all excellent choices. Basically, having a varied, balanced diet will keep you healthy.

A Final Word on Food

It is important not to become too strict with yourself or overzealous in following your diet. The main thing is for you to make a healthy diet a part of your lifestyle. If you do that and stick with it, you will feel the results of your efforts.

Exercise

Exercise is perhaps the best stress-reduction technique of all, and that includes the physical and emotional stress associated with PMS. Premenstrual syndrome can make your body and mind feel drained. Exercise helps your body release the pain and stress that is making you feel tired and down. As a result, after exercising you will feel far more energized and comfortable. Exercise causes the

Lifestyle Changes

release of the brain's "feel good" chemicals that act as natural painkillers and mood enhancers. It helps loosen up your muscles, even your cramping abdominal muscles. A good workout also helps you to sleep longer and more deeply, something that is not always easy to do when you are experiencing PMS. Chances are you will be in less pain and will feel more rested after exercise. Your mood will have improved dramatically also after exercising.

Aside from its PMS-related benefits, exercise can have a positive influence on your health in general. If you exercise regularly, you will have an easier time keeping weight off. Your cholesterol levels, muscle tone, and flexibility will all improve. It will give a boost to your immune system, allowing you to better fight off diseases, infections, viruses, and the effects of stress. Exercise even makes it easier to try to quit smoking and overeating. Exercise helps to increase blood flow to your brain, bringing with it sugars and oxygen that you need in order to think clearly and work hard. This increased blood flow also removes toxins in your brain that collect and that make it hard for you to concentrate and to solve problems.

A word of caution: If you are not yet in good shape, don't try to start your exercise routine when you feel early signs of PMS. Instead start your program the first day you notice PMS waning. By the time your next period comes, you will be in better shape and will be better able to fight the symptoms of PMS. When you do start exercising, don't overdo it. Give yourself small, attainable goals at first. For example, if you choose jogging and do it for forty-five minutes one day, you may not be able to walk the next day, much less exercise. Better to start out with a ten-minute run one day and increase your time to fifteen minutes the next week.

Coping with PMS (Premenstrual Syndrome)

Whatever you do, make sure stretching is part of your workout. Stretch before and after you exercise. It helps to relax the body and can help prevent injury.

Another idea for making exercise work for you is to vary your activities and break them up into smaller parts. If the idea of a forty-minute run or swim seems outrageous, try breaking the time into fifteen or twenty-minute segments. For example, you could take the dog for a fifteen-minute walk before school and then jump rope for fifteen minutes before dinner. Basically, any type of movement will make you feel better both mentally and physically.

In case you need help in deciding what might turn you on to exercise, here are some of the best aerobic exercises:

Aerobics
This category includes aerobic dance and step aerobics, which you can do in a class or by yourself in your own home with videotapes, television programs, or whatever kind of music you like. Just turn up the music and dance!

Biking
Riding a bike outdoors has been an option since the first ones were invented in the early 1800s. In recent years, exercise (stationary) bikes have popped up everywhere—in homes, athletic clubs, recreation centers, and gyms.

Cross-Country Skiing
In the past you had to live in the mountains to enjoy this exhilarating activity, and then only in winter. Now with exercise machines, you can "ski" at home or in a gym.

Lifestyle Changes

Jogging
For some people, jogging produces a "runner's high" they do not get from anything else. This is thought to be the result of the brain's production of endorphins—natural euphorics and painkillers—during sustained aerobic activity. If you live in a warm community, jogging may work for you year-round, as long as you don't have bad knees. To preserve your knees, try to alternate jogging with another, less-jarring activity.

Jumping Rope and Jumping Jacks
You can alternate these two activities and include a third—trampoline jumping or minitramp jumping. Turn on some wild music and get going. Because your jump rope will not take up much room in a suitcase, the first two activities can be done even if you are traveling.

Walking
Walking is an exercise that costs nothing, that requires no special clothing or equipment (other than comfortable shoes), and that can be done easily every day. As you stroll, listen to music through your headphones or just enjoy nature or your neighborhood. If you prefer indoor walking, you can use a track or a treadmill, or go to the mall and enjoy some brisk window shopping.

Anything that gets you moving can improve your mood and can encourage a more healthy lifestyle. Don't forget to record the time, date, and type of exercise in your journal or on your PMS chart.

Other Lifestyle Changes

Sleep is a great PMS fighter; the trouble is that insomnia and sleep disturbances may be annoying symptoms. Lack of sleep can make you crabby, another PMS symptom. Being overtired only makes matters worse. To help reduce the fatigue, pain, and moodiness of PMS, it is important to go to bed and get up at about the same time every day. This helps keep your body's inner "clock" running smoothly. If you are overtired and have an irregular sleep schedule, this clock gets out of whack. The result is that production of your brain's natural "feel-good chemicals"—those chemicals that fight stress, let you enjoy a deep and restful sleep, boost your energy, relieve pain, and increase pleasure—goes down.

Sleep

Here are two important words about sleep. Do it! For a restful sleep, take a hot bath, then curl up under the covers with a heating pad (if you need it) and a good book. Try to go to bed at about the same time each night and get up about the same time each morning. If you do take naps, make them very short (ten minutes or less). And remember: Try not to have caffeine after 3 PM, or better yet, have no caffeine at all. Exercise as early in the day as possible. Don't exercise just before bedtime; instead of making you tired, exercise at this time will probably make you feel wired.

Some people worry about lack of sleep, and the worrying makes their insomnia worse. Studies have shown that most people do not need as much sleep as they think. In general, young people need more sleep than older people. But seven to nine hours of sleep each night should be enough. You will probably be able to figure out what seems right for you.

Lifestyle Changes

If you have insomnia, try spending less time in bed. Loretta used to go to bed every night at 10 PM because everyone else in her family did. During her PMS phase, she spent the first hour tossing and turning and worrying that she was not sleeping. These days she writes in her journal until 10:30 or 10:45. Then she listens to some soft music and is usually sound asleep before 11:00 PM.

Light

Many women say their mood improves when they get outside and experience the healing effects of the sun. These observations are beginning to be proven through science. A 1997 study conducted by the Royal Postgraduate Medical School in London, England, found that fifteen- to twenty-minute daily treatments with a flashing light device greatly reduced the symptoms of PMS. After three months of this light stimulation therapy, the average reduction in symptoms among the seventeen participating women was 76 percent. Twelve of the seventeen women were considered to be no longer suffering from PMS after the three-month study period. Researchers theorize that PMS may be a brainwave disorder (which they also suspect is the cause of attention deficit disorder and chronic fatigue syndrome) that can be corrected with the stimulating effect of light.

To enjoy the PMS-fighting benefits of light, instead of jumping in the car every time you want to go somewhere, try walking or biking. The exercise will help, and so will the sun. Be sure to use sunscreen with SPF 15 or higher on all exposed areas of the skin. A word of warning: Don't assume that if sunlight helps PMS moods, a tanning salon will work better. High concentrations of ultraviolet light are hard on the skin and are a potential cause of skin cancer.

Coping with PMS (Premenstrual Syndrome)

Stress

The word itself, with its hissing "s" sounds, has a terrible ring. STRESS. Believe it or not, stress in your life comes not only from difficult times but from happy experiences as well. To check out the truth of the latter statement, just ask someone who has planned a wedding.

What is stress? The word originated in physics; it refers to the ability to withstand strain. Stress causes your body to pour out adrenaline, a chemical that readies you for the "fight or flight" response. This is a useful response if someone is chasing you down a dark alley or holding you up. But the body cannot withstand permanent stress (fast breathing, sweating, high blood pressure, muscle contraction) for very long. Stress can push you beyond your usual coping abilities. We all have stress in our lives. Too much time on our hands or not enough; pressures of school, job, and family; relationships with self or friends—at times these concerns can push us to the breaking point. Add the stress of PMS, and you may feel like you can't take much more.

One of the first things you can do to relieve stress is to try to figure out the causes. Keeping your PMS chart should help. Is PMS itself the major stressor? Or is something else, such as your parents' divorce or separation, your own relationship breakup, a move to a new town or school, or upcoming final exams, the major stressor? You have no control over many of the events that intrude in your life. You can try to control how you react to some of them.

You can help yourself and your reactions by changing the way you think. Psychologists who prescribe these kinds of changes call them cognitive therapy. Sometimes this method is called positive thinking.

Lifestyle Changes

Dr. David Burns, the author of many books on depression, self-esteem, and mental health, generally receives credit for popularizing cognitive distortions, or irrational and illogical thinking that can cause stress, low self-esteem, and depression. The following distortions are adapted from a list in *The Wellness Book* by Herbert Benson, Eileen M. Stuart, and associates at the Mind/Body Medical Institute.

1. **"Should" statements.** Constantly telling yourself, "I should have a healthy diet," or "I should exercise" is a recipe for emotional burnout. Other people don't like to hear you say what they should do, and you don't like to hear other people tell you what you should do. Why force "should" statements on yourself? Instead say, "I choose to eat a healthful diet," or "I want to exercise."

2. **Labeling**. If you make a mistake or an error in judgment, say so. "I made a mistake." Don't say, "I'm a dummy" or "I'm so stupid" (because you're not).

3. **Personalization and blame.** A medication or a treatment you are trying for PMS does not work. You assume responsibility for this as if you single-handedly have made your body unresponsive to the new treatment. If you are going to personalize, it is better to give yourself credit for trying something new.

4. **Magnification**. You turn a negative happening or event into something world shattering. For example, you complain that PMS is the worst thing that ever happened to anyone, that you can't stand it, etc. Remember that PMS is not a life-threatening condition. Yes, it is a pain, but you can stand it.

5. **Overgeneralization**. You see one aspect of your life as part of an ongoing pattern of defeat. You have PMS; therefore, your life is ruined. Wrong. Your life is not ruined. You are coping with a troublesome condition as best you can, and you will continue to do so.

6. **Discounting the positive**. Many people are guilty of this one. Someone compliments you on your sweater. You say, "Oh, I've had this thing for years." No! Thank them and let it go at that. As far as PMS is concerned, some young women focus on the negative (the effects of PMS) and forget all the good things going on in their lives.

7. **Emotional reasoning**. You assume that the way you are feeling on a down day is evidence of the truth. For example, you feel rather powerless on a PMS day, and you say to yourself, "I'm a worthless person."

Ways to Reduce Stress

What relieves stress for one person may cause stress for another. Dianna likes to have at least one weekend day in which she does basically nothing. She sleeps until noon, gets up and makes pancakes for breakfast, talks to her friends on the phone, reads, and does homework. In the evening, she watches television or a movie and has a bowl of popcorn. On some of these days, Dianna does not even leave the house, except maybe to rent a movie. By the next day, she's full of energy and ready to face the world.

Vanessa would feel depressed after a day like Dianna's. She would consider such a day wasteful and get stressed out about it. Vanessa likes to get up early and go for a jog

Lifestyle Changes

with one of her friends. After that they sometimes watch a movie or ride their bikes to the mall. After lunch on Saturdays, Vanessa does four hours of volunteer work at the local children's hospital. Before getting on the phone to make plans for the evening, Vanessa cleans her room. She knows her mom will not let her go out until she does. Dianna would feel horrible after a day like Vanessa's. Her stress level would reach unimaginable heights. Obviously, the two have different ways of dealing with stress.

Since we have already discussed exercise, a few more words may wrap it up. Exercise is without question a stress reliever. What felt annoying yesterday does not seem to bother you today after ten minutes of jumping jacks. The only circumstance in which exercise might cause stress is when a person becomes compulsive about doing it. "My daughter got that way about swimming," says Michaela's mother. "If she couldn't have her daily swim, she got irritable. If we were on a family trip, we had to stay at a place with a pool. She exercised too much. It was unhealthy."

There are some other stress busters that may or may not work for you. Try them for several months, all month, not just during PMS time.

Seek Silence

For most people, constant loud noise is a stressor. Often we have no choice about the noise that assaults us—from the music in the supermarket or the coffee shop to street sounds, like horns, motorcycles, buses, and trucks. If you live in the city, try to get away every so often. But a trip to the mountains, the country, or the seashore may not be possible often enough. If you cannot get away, find quiet time wherever you are. You may find your quiet time in the morning before everyone else gets up or at night after everyone else is asleep. Finding a quiet, pretty place to go in times of stress can be very helpful.

Find Your Own Place
Everyone needs a place to call his or her own. If you have your own room, make this area truly yours. Turn your room into a place where you want to hang out, a place that pleases you. Choose colors and a decor that feels restful and stress-free. Decorate it with your kind of art and give it your own personal touch.

Even if you do not have your own room, you can still find a corner to make "your" place. If you have to share a room, see if you can schedule some private time when only you are allowed in. Or find another place in your home where you can have peace and quiet.

Deep Breathing
Deep breathing is a common relaxation technique, one that many cultures have practiced for thousands of years as a necessary first step to spiritual enlightenment. Taking a few deep breaths at various times throughout the day is a great way to become instantly relaxed. You can do it anywhere and anytime: after the alarm clock wakes you up, after you get out of the shower, just before walking into school, while waiting on the lunch line, on the bus ride home, or just before you go to sleep.

Begin by closing your eyes. Let your body go limp. Close your mouth and breathe deeply through your nose until it feels like your lungs cannot hold any more air. Hold the breath for several seconds and then slowly release it.

Lifestyle Changes

You can repeat this several times in one session, but don't overdo it; you may begin to hyperventilate.

Can't you already feel the tension and discomfort flowing out of your body? Just one deep breath will make your heart slow down, your blood pressure decrease, and your blood become filled with energizing oxygen. Taking several deep-breathing breaks during your busy day is a far better way to release stress and gain energy than is a coffee or junk food snack break.

Progressive Muscle Relaxation

One of the most common effects of stress on your body is tense muscles. Muscles that become tight in your back and neck can lead to serious backaches and headaches. When your body is in pain, you can become even more stressed, which means your body can become even more tight and painful. It is a vicious cycle.

One way to break the cycle is to practice progressive muscle relaxation. This involves first tensing your muscles for five seconds and then letting them go slack and releasing all tension. By tensing the muscles first, the feeling of relief is greater when you let them relax. Sit in a comfortable chair or lie down on a bed or on the floor. Close your eyes and focus on what parts of your body feel especially tense. There are fifteen muscle groups you should tense and relax. Tense and release each of these groups of muscles in the following order:

- Right hand and forearm
- Right bicep
- Left hand and forearm

Coping with PMS (Premenstrual Syndrome)

- Left bicep
- Forehead
- Cheeks and nose
- Mouth
- Neck and shoulders
- Chest and stomach
- Right thigh
- Right foot and calf
- Right toes
- Left thigh
- Left foot and calf
- Left toes

After each tensing, enjoy the feeling of relaxation that follows. Focus on the tension that is leaving your body. When you have completed tensing and releasing each muscle group, lie or sit still for a few minutes to bask in the new stillness and relaxation. Take several deep breaths to complete the process and prepare yourself to return to your busy life.

You can also use muscle relaxation at any time during the day to concentrate on specific areas of tension. If you feel like your neck and shoulders are tightening up, take a moment to relax those muscles. You may prevent the onset of a stress headache and other PMS symptoms.

Lifestyle Changes

Massage

Massage relaxes muscles and decreases stress. As her first symptom of PMS, Linda often feels a tightness in her neck muscles. Sometimes she tries to give her own neck a massage, but twisting herself into a pretzel hurts more than it helps. Getting a friend to rub her neck is much nicer. It is not hard to learn massage. You can get a book on massage from the library. Then you and a friend can take turns. If you save your money, you can go to a certified massage therapist for a relaxing treat.

Meditation

Meditation is another excellent way to relieve stress and pain. Sit still and concentrate very hard. Focus all of your thoughts on just one thing, such as your breathing. Start with ten minutes and work up to twenty. Stop thinking about the problems that are causing stress. As a result, your body will relax, and by the end of your meditation session, you will feel refreshed and more optimistic and calm.

Find a comfortable position in a quiet room. You might sit on a straight chair with your feet on the floor and your hands on your thighs. Begin by taking a few deep breaths, holding them, and releasing them slowly. Then focus on something simple, like the rhythm of your own heartbeat, a physical object that pleases you (flowers, candle flame, painting, or photo), or the silent repetition of a word or a sound. You can also visualize a beautiful and soothing place in your mind and imagine you are there. Or you can imagine good health and relaxation entering your body with each breath you take, and illness and tension leaving with each breath you release. Whatever technique you use, it is important to

Coping with PMS (Premenstrual Syndrome)

block out all other sights, sounds, and troubling thoughts or distractions. If you notice that worries are creeping into your thoughts, ignore them and refocus on your one sound, image, or object. Soon your body will begin to relax and a soothing feeling will wash over you.

Visualization
Use your deep breathing to start the exercise of visualization. Then close your eyes and use your imagination to create a mental picture. You probably already use visualization without realizing that you are practicing a potentially healing art. You may have imagined a teacher handing back a test and announcing, "You have the highest grade in the class. Congratulations!"

You can use visualization to displace some of the stress caused by PMS. If you feel discomfort in your pelvic area, imagine the blood flowing away from your pelvis and being replaced by a calm and relaxed feeling. Imagine yourself in a bubbly mood. You feel light, hopeful, and energetic. You are in control of whatever problem presents itself. Imagine yourself smiling and people smiling back at you. Your visualizations are limited only by your imagination, and your imagination knows no limits.

Yoga
The practice of yoga, joining mind and body, is something you can do alone once you get the hang of it. But you will probably do best if you start by taking a class. Yoga incorporates stretching, breathing, and meditation for relaxation and healing. The Eastern practice of Hatha yoga, based on physical movements called asanas and breathing exercises (pranayama) is commonly taught in the United States.

Lifestyle Changes

Other Eastern practices, such as tai chi, involve rhythmic movements that help fight stress. Taoist and Buddhist monks developed tai chi hundreds of years ago as a martial art and a spiritual discipline. Because the movements are slow and meditative, they are suitable for all fitness levels. Among the benefits of tai chi are improved circulation, increased balance and flexibility, and inner peace.

Biofeedback

Biofeedback is sometimes used for high levels of stress. It requires training and involves the use of electronic machinery to help you control physiological responses. This, in turn, helps you to control stress. Electronic devices are connected to the body and the signals are seen on a screen. In this way, a person can learn to control internal, unseen physical responses, such as heart rate and blood pressure.

Although no controlled research has yet been published on the effectiveness of biofeedback for treating PMS, some clinical studies have shown that it can be helpful in alleviating both the physical and the emotional symptoms. Women who try biofeedback as a treatment for PMS usually receive twenty to thirty training sessions. One biofeedback provider in California reports that 90 percent of its PMS patients achieve a "favorable outcome" as a result of their training, which means their PMS symptoms no longer disrupt daily activities or relationships. Some patients have reported becoming symptom-free for many months and even years.

Biofeedback takes a long time to learn. It may be a while before you can regulate your responses. You can practice at home without the machines. If you keep practicing, you may be able to cut down on stress, muscle tension, headaches, and insomnia. In addition, you will have gained

Coping with PMS (Premenstrual Syndrome)

a feeling of control over your physical and emotional health, one of your primary goals in dealing with PMS.

Raising Your Own Self-Esteem

Self-esteem (the ability to think well of yourself) is a characteristic that develops over the years, partially as a result of the ways you were raised. Although there is no way a person can choose his or her parents, there are ways you can raise your self-esteem. One way is to step out of the "I'm a bad person" mentality and start thinking of yourself as good and valuable—not because of anything you have done, but just because you are. The affirmation exercise below is one thing you can do. Then when you start getting down on yourself, take out your list and study it.

Remember: Those who brag the most or spend the most time talking about themselves are not necessarily those with the highest level of self-esteem. Natalie has an example: "In my senior year of high school, I started dating this guy named Joe. You know the type—captain of the football team, class president, and really good looking. But the only person he ever talked about was himself. He never seemed to care about how I was feeling. In the middle of the year, this new girl came to our school. I'd invited Joe to the Sadie Hawkins Dance, but he broke up with me two days before the dance and went with her, leaving me with a new dress and no date. I look back and ask myself, 'Did he have high self-esteem or low?' I have to say, low. People with high self-esteem are confident but considerate of other people, not just themselves." Having high self-esteem will help you fight off some of the depression, anxiety, irritability, and other mood changes that often appear with PMS.

Lifestyle Changes

Affirmations

Affirmations are positive statements you make to yourself about yourself. You can say them or write them. Begin with the words "I am." The use of affirmations will help pull you out of a low period and the negative-thinking mode that sometimes accompanies PMS. Here are a few samples:

- I am a healthy person.
- I am a whole person.
- I am athletic.
- I am artistic.
- I am fun to be around.
- I am competent.
- I am in charge of my own life.

Don't allow negative thoughts to creep in. Just for fun, time yourself. See how many affirmations you can write in five minutes. Then whenever you feel down, read them back to yourself. Or you can read them into a tape recorder and play them back. Better yet, write them on a piece of poster board and hang it over your desk.

Be Assertive

Many people confuse assertiveness with aggressiveness. They are not the same. Aggressiveness has a negative connotation because aggression can often cause harm to another person. Assertiveness is different. The dictionary defines an assertion as something stated forcefully. Being assertive allows you to express your feelings while at the same time respecting the rights and feelings of others. As harmless and useful as this sounds, many men (and even other women) do not expect women to be assertive. The negative side of this passivity or nonassertiveness is that you do not get heard. When no one listens to you, you are likely to develop feelings of resentment, anger, and even depression.

Be Forgiving: Don't Hold a Grudge

How does forgiveness fit with PMS? Forgiveness is important in the same way that expressing your opinions and needs is important. It is important in much the same way as dealing with anger is important. If you don't let go of feelings of resentment, they will eat away at you. Forgiveness promotes the mental health of the person who does the forgiving.

In her book *Forgiving the Unforgivable: Overcoming the Bitter Legacy of Intimate Wounds*, Beverly Flanigan lists five phases leading to forgiveness.

> **Phase 1: Naming the Injury.** This involves figuring out the significance of the act to you. In Natalie's family, a cardinal rule was, "Honor your obligations to others." Whether her boyfriend wanted to go to the Sadie Hawkins Dance with her was not the point. Natalie believed that because he had accepted her invitation, he should have gone to the dance with her no matter what. He could have broken up with her later.

Lifestyle Changes

Phase 2: Claiming the Injury. In this phase, Natalie admits that her feelings were hurt. She has no date to the dance and is stuck with a new dress she cannot return.

Phase 3: Blaming the Injury. The fact is, Joe is to blame for breaking the date. The responsibility is his. His new date is not to blame.

Phase 4: Balancing the Scales. Flanigan says this phase allows the act of forgiveness to begin. Natalie did not cause the pain, but she has pain. If she continues to lick her wounds, she will not be able to move on. If, however, she acknowledges her position of strength as a person with a clear conscience, she will be able to begin to move to a new place of forgiveness.

Phase 5: Choosing to Forgive. Realizing that negative feelings will eat away at her, Natalie makes the choice to forgive—for her own good, if for no other reason. The pain that is still there will heal with time.

Keeping a Journal

How many people do you know who keep a journal—one that they do not have to keep for a class, that is. It was once very common for men and women to make daily entries in journals, but the practice is dying out. Edward Robb Ellis kept a daily journal for sixty-eight years, beginning when he was sixteen. He and a friend agreed to keep journals for a year without missing a day. The friend quit, but Ellis kept going; he published *A Diary of the Century* in 1995. Recording your thoughts and feelings is a creative act, a stress reliever, and a valuable record of

Coping with PMS (Premenstrual Syndrome)

your life—even if you do not become America's greatest diarist. Julia Cameron, author of *The Artist's Way*, believes that keeping a journal is a way to recover a sense of power, strength, and connection to others.

Laugh a Little, Laugh a Lot!

According to *The Wellness Book*, Dr. Barry Greiff, a psychiatrist, is credited for emphasizing the stress-busting properties of the "five Ls of success." These are:

Learning Throughout your whole life, not just during your school years

Laboring Working at something you love and that gives meaning to your life

Loving Giving and receiving love

Letting go Let go of the "shoulds" and all the other things that are out of your control

and finally, **Laughter**

Over the years many experts have attested to the healing power of laughter. Pat O'Brien, MSW, is one of these experts. O'Brien is the founder and director of You Gotta Believe! The Older Child Adoption and Permanency Movement, Inc., a child placement agency in Brooklyn, New York, that finds permanent homes for teenagers in foster care. O'Brien urges people to "play, participate, and have phun." Humor is an individual matter, he says, and we all need to get in touch with the special things that

Lifestyle Changes

make us laugh. He offers a twelve-step approach to "Independent Laughing," a way of getting in touch with your own special brand of humor.

O'Brien gives credit to C. W. Metcalf and Roma Felible *(Lighten Up: Survival Skills for People Under Pressure)* for the idea of a "Joy List." You can keep a list or journal of your life's joys in conjunction with your PMS journal or chart. Keeping a journal of happy times will help you remember that life is good and—most of the time—fun. Here is an entry from Becky's Joy Journal.

> *"When I was really young, we were on a camping trip in Mexico. It was close to dinnertime, and I was starving. I noticed a couple of pieces of cheese on a paper plate. Before anyone could see me, I grabbed a piece and stuffed it in my face. The 'cheese' turned out to be a chunk of yellow soap. When I started foaming at the mouth, everybody started laughing. At the time I felt humiliated. But now when I think back to that incident, all the happy memories of my family and our camping trip flood over me, and I laugh, too."*

In their book, *The Laughter Prescription*, Dr. Laurence J. Peter and Bill Dana give many reasons why laughter, even in this age of high technology and scientific breakthroughs, is the best medicine. Some believe laughter increases the production of endorphins, the body's natural painkillers. Laughing also draws attention away from pain and reduces muscle tension. Add to laughter an ability to see humor in many situations, and you have a prescription for healing.

Other Creative Activities

Anything that lifts you out of yourself—or, on the other hand, gets you deeply into yourself—can provide relief from the low-down feelings of PMS. These creative activities are as unique as the individuals who do them. What gives you a sense of peace and fulfillment? Writing poetry or short stories? Dancing? Painting? Drawing? Making music? Cooking? Dress designing? Gardening? The possibilities are endless.

The Mind-Body and Body-Mind Connection

As you know, PMS is different for each woman who has it. Symptoms of backache, headache, joint discomfort, and muscle stiffness (to name a few) involve pain. Other physical symptoms (diarrhea or constipation, for example) are uncomfortable and can produce a great deal of misery. Finally, emotional symptoms, such as angry outbursts, intense sadness, or crying spells, can influence your bodily reactions. In some situations, the mind influences the body; in others, the body influences the mind and emotions.

In her book, *Managing Pain Before It Manages You*, Margaret Caudill writes that your first step in managing pain is to acknowledge that it exists. After you do that, check with yourself to see if you are taking ownership of your discomfort, or if you are blaming others for your pain. Dr. Caudill points out that some women blame their doctors (e.g., "Why can't he or she cure it?"). Others blame

Lifestyle Changes

family members for not doing anything that helps or for not understanding the situation. Still others blame society for their circumstances, for not making things easier for them.

Becky blamed her parents for her PMS discomfort. Backaches and lower abdominal pain were part of Becky's PMS picture. "The least you could do is let me drive to school when my back is killing me," Becky said.

"Why don't you try walking to school," said her mom. "It's not that far, and the exercise would be good for you."

"Sure, Mom," Becky said. "Sure." To herself she said, "If I don't graduate this year, my parents will have themselves to blame."

Becky refused to try her mother's advice (she got a ride to school with a friend or stayed home on the couch) and, as a result, lost a possible symptom-reliever. She nursed angry feelings toward her parents that made her discomfort worse. In addition, through her lack of action, Becky gave control and responsibility for her pain to her innocent parents.

Becky's story has a happy ending. She did graduate from high school and moved on to college. In the middle of her freshman year, she made friends with another young woman who had PMS. Becky's friend, Char, didn't try to talk Becky into anything. But one day, Becky noticed Char's swimsuit hanging in her bathroom and asked how often she swam.

"Every day," said Char, "especially when I'm PMS-ing. It helps. Want to come?"

Coping with PMS (Premenstrual Syndrome)

> *Becky had a flashback to her mom's offering of exercise suggestions and almost didn't go. However, rather than saying to herself, "I should go," she said, "I want to go."*
>
> *Afterward, instead of staying home on the sofa on PMS days, Becky made the extra effort to swim, which relieved much of her discomfort. "Mom was right about exercise," Becky said to herself as she did her laps. "I hate to admit it, but she was right."*

All the lifestyle changes described in this chapter are part of the mind-body link that many researchers are exploring today. If you have ever felt as if you might faint when giving an oral book report, or if you have broken out in hives before a big test or have gotten a migraine after Christmas shopping, you know firsthand how your emotions can influence your body. In the same way, what happens in your body can affect your mind and your emotions. For example, if having PMS causes you to give up, you are letting your body influence your mind. Mind and body are two different entities, but in reality they cannot be separated. Understanding the connection is the first step in dealing with PMS. The more you know, the better you will feel.

Do You Need More Help?

No one knows why one young woman gets PMS and another does not. Premenstrual syndrome is a complex condition, and it is different in each person. But when you are the one who is suffering, you need more than just comforting words.

If the lifestyle changes you have made seem not to have made enough of a difference, you may decide to consult a doctor. Even if the doctor's remedies do not work, you will have reassured yourself that you do not have a life-threatening condition or one that may later lead to difficulties.

Choosing a Medical Practitioner

As PMS has become more accepted by the medical community, the need for specialty clinics may have lessened. In other words, your own doctor may know more about its treatment than doctors did in the past. But you still may be able to find a clinic in your community devoted only to PMS. Specialized resources are listed at the end of this book.

Some young women have gone to the same doctor since they were babies. If that is your situation, you are lucky. Over the years, you and your pediatrician or family physician have probably developed a close relationship.

Coping with PMS (Premenstrual Syndrome)

If you are starting from scratch and do not know any doctors, talk to your friends. See if you can find a physician who specializes in the problems of young women, specifically those with menstrual disorders. If you are in high school, you may have access to a school-based clinic. If you live near a large hospital, you may find a PMS expert at a clinic that specializes in treating adolescent patients.

Your family's health plan may limit your choices. If you have severe PMS or a related condition, your primary care physician may refer you to a gynecologist, a doctor who specializes in treating conditions of the female reproductive system. (Many women see a gynecologist as their only doctor.) You may also see a nurse practitioner (a nurse with extra training who performs many of the functions of a doctor) or a certified nurse midwife (CNM). Both of the latter work in cooperation with a physician. More and more doctors are forming teams that may consist of nurse practitioners, nurse midwives, and physician assistants, who help with patient education and the prevention of certain health problems.

If you feel more comfortable with a female health provider, request one. Also try to schedule your appointment for after your period ends but before new PMS symptoms begin. That way you will have a more rational outlook on the problem.

Maybe going to a doctor is something you would never do on your own. But one day, your mother says, "I'm going to pick you up early from school on Thursday. We have an appointment with Dr. Perkins."

"But, Mom . . ."

Do You Need More Help?

When you feel angry, irritable, or depressed, the people around you are affected, too. Your mom wants to help you, which in turn will help relieve her concerns. She may worry that something is seriously wrong with you. It is her job as a mother to get the best treatment she can find for you. It is possible that she also has PMS. Or maybe she has never had such problems and cannot understand why you do. For whatever reason, it is a good idea to talk to your doctor. You can help yourself and put your mom's mind at ease.

What You Can Do

Be aware of your rights and responsibilities as a patient. One of your responsibilities is to understand that your doctor is not only trying to identify your problem but also to rule out anything more serious. Although PMS can cause major distress, it is not life-threatening. And although you have come to the doctor because of PMS, your specialist or family doctor will probably do a full physical, not just a pelvic examination.

If you have a close relationship with your mother, you might appreciate her support during the exam. You do have a right, however, to ask your doctor to keep confidential certain parts of your history (such as sexual activity).

Part of the physical should be a breast examination. If you tell the doctor that you perform regular breast self-exams, he or she will be impressed. He or she will check your breasts by observation and will feel them for lumps. Although it is unlikely that the doctor will find anything, he or she is showing you how to do what we discussed in chapter 1. All women need to perform breast self-exams regularly.

The Pelvic Exam

In trying to rule out other conditions, the doctor may decide that a pelvic examination is in order. Your first "pelvic" is one of those initiation rites into womanhood. Candice says, "I thought the start of menstruation was my initiation into womanhood. Now a second one?"

If your doctor is male, a female nurse or other chaperone is also usually present for the exam. The doctor will ask you to lie down on the examining table and put your feet in stirrups. Although this position may be awkward, uncomfortable, and embarrassing for you at first, it is all in a day's work for the doctor. He or she cannot check your female organs when you are standing up. And remember that your anatomy looks very much like the thousands of others the doctor sees each year. To check the vagina, the cervix, and the uterus, the doctor will insert a speculum to separate the vaginal walls. Next he or she will probably take a scraping from the cervix for a Papanicolaou, or "Pap," test to screen for cancer or precancerous conditions.

The examination is short and will soon be done. This may be the time for you to use creative visualizations (imagine yourself at the seashore or hiking a snow-covered mountain). Because he or she cannot see the rest of your uterus or your ovaries, the doctor will feel them by inserting two gloved and lubricated fingers into the vagina. Sometimes a final procedure is a rectal exam in which the doctor makes an additional check of the internal reproductive organs with a finger in the rectum and a hand on the abdomen.

Your doctor may want to see the results of any laboratory tests before discussing her findings with you. The tests are unlikely to reveal any pathology (disease), and your doctor

Do You Need More Help?

may confirm what you thought all along: You have PMS. Once that fact is established, you will be able to make a plan with your doctor that includes anything you have already tried (that helped) along with treatments she suggests.

If you are sexually active, you should begin yearly pelvic examinations now. If you are not sexually active and your PMS symptoms are mild, you can ask your family doctor when you should start seeing a gynecologist.

What the Doctor Wants to Hear from You

At some time during your appointment, be sure the doctor hears what you have to say. Be honest. Your doctor is a smart person with many years of training and experience, but he or she cannot read your mind or know your feelings about your symptoms unless you speak up. In the treatment of PMS, a patient report is vitally important because of the likelihood that nothing will show up on the physical exam.

Your doctor may want to know whether you are ovulating. This information will be valuable in figuring out whether you have PMS. (If you are not ovulating, you probably do not have PMS.) You can track ovulation using measurements of your daily body temperature upon waking. A woman's body temperature rises at ovulation. Before you get up in the morning, record your temperature on your PMS chart.

Be ready to answer these questions: What are your symptoms? When during your menstrual cycle do you have them? How severe are the symptoms? How long do they last? Do they stop when your period starts? What self-help measures have you tried? What has worked and what has not worked? Has another doctor ever prescribed treatments such as birth control pills? If so, what kind and what

Coping with PMS (Premenstrual Syndrome)

dosage? Do you have any other symptoms that may or may not be part of the PMS picture? Did your mother or your grandmother have PMS? If you suffer from depression, how bad is it? Do other family members get depressed?

Because you know yourself better than anyone else, there is much you can do to help the doctor make a diagnosis. Your journal or PMS chart is important. Be sure to take it with you.

Possible Treatments

In addition to the remedies you have tried on your own (lowering or eliminating caffeine; limiting salt intake; avoiding alcohol; eating lots of fruits, vegetables, and complex carbohydrates; exercising; reducing stress), your doctor may prescribe some kind of medication. If the prescribed treatment does not make sense to you, say so. After all, it is your body.

None of the treatments below help all women, and scientific studies have not shown any one treatment to be better than all others. Nevertheless, some women report that their PMS symptoms respond to one or more of these remedies.

Vitamins and Minerals
If you eat a well-balanced diet and include the PMS-fighting foods mentioned earlier, your body may not need additional vitamins. However, some people need more vitamins or minerals than do others. Deficiencies of magnesium, manganese, calcium, B vitamins, vitamin E, and linoleic acid have been reported in some women with PMS and menstrual discomfort. Therefore, some

Do You Need More Help?

doctors tell their patients to take a multivitamin tablet every day or prescribe a combination vitamin-mineral pill. Taking vitamin and mineral supplements, as directed by a doctor, has been shown to improve some PMS symptoms. The following are recommended daily dosages of the five vitamins and minerals thought to be most effective in alleviating PMS symptoms:

- Calcium: 1,000 mg

- Magnesium: 400 mg

- Manganese: 6 mg

- Vitamin E: 400 IU

- Vitamin B_6: 100mg

B_6 (pyridoxine) is the most commonly prescribed vitamin for PMS. It is one of the complex B vitamins. It is thought that B_6 helps the body to synthesize catecholamine, a type of neurotransmitter. As we have seen, neurotransmitters help to fight depression, anxiety, difficulty concentrating, and other emotional problems. If the doctor prescribes vitamin B_6 in the form of tablets, be absolutely sure not to take a higher dose than prescribed. As with most medications, more is not necessarily better and can be dangerous. In the case of B_6, an overdose can cause serious sensory neuropathy (nerve injury resulting in numbness, weakness, burning, and pain) in the hands and feet. Other undesirable side effects are headaches, disturbed sleep, dizziness, and nausea. Taking B_6 with food should also prevent stomach upset.

Coping with PMS (Premenstrual Syndrome)

Though B_6 has been used to treat PMS for years in both Europe and the United States, the results of scientific studies have failed to prove its effectiveness conclusively. A 1998 study found use of B_6 to be no more effective in treating PMS symptoms than a placebo (a fake pill made of sugar, used to create a control group). Some researchers believe that the combination of B_6 and magnesium may be more effective than taking either one alone.

Magnesium, if taken from the fifteenth day of the menstrual cycle (fifteen days after period bleeding begins) to the beginning of the next period, seems to help improve premenstrual mood swings. Some studies also indicate that it may help reduce fluid retention, weight gain, breast tenderness, and abdominal bloating. The daily recommended dosage of magnesium is 400 mg, but for PMS the amount is often boosted to 500–1,000 mg daily from the fifteenth day of the menstrual cycle to the first day of the period. This dosage should be safe for most women, but you should always check with your doctor before taking any vitamin or mineral supplements, especially if you have any medical problems.

Some foods that are high in B_6 are salmon, tuna, shrimp, and chicken. Grains such as whole wheat, rice bran, and rye are good sources of the vitamin B complex. Additional sources are soybeans, navy beans, lima beans, and pinto beans. In other words, if you eat a diet high in complex carbohydrates, you will be getting lots of multiple B vitamins.

A 1998 Columbia University study found that women who took 300 mg of calcium four times a day had a reduction in mood swings, pain, bloating, depression, back pain, and food cravings. This should be a safe dosage for most women, but consult your doctor before taking calcium supplements.

Do You Need More Help?

Both vitamin E and manganese are thought by many to be effective in treating some of the symptoms of PMS, but the evidence from studies thus far is weak.

Be sure to use these vitamin and mineral supplements under a physician's direction. Too high a dose can be dangerous, especially for people with other medical problems.

Herbal Remedies

In recent years, the popularity of alternative, or nontraditional, medicine has skyrocketed. Every year, Americans spend about $30 billion on alternative treatments and medication. Herbal supplements, which are becoming more and more popular every year, are responsible for much of this increase in popularity. Americans now spend about $4 billion on herbal supplements annually. Because these products are derived from herbs and are labeled "all-natural," many consumers assume they are safe. This is not always the case. The federal government does not currently have the same power to regulate herbal supplements that it does to ensure the safety of prescription and over-the-counter drugs. As a result, the herbal supplements industry has few standards and poor quality control, often makes misleading health claims for its products, and frequently provides inadequate ingredient lists and information about possible negative effects.

Any herbal supplements you buy should not be taken until you have read the ingredient list and instructions carefully and have shown the package to your doctor to receive her or his opinion on the safety and effectiveness of the medication.

Some popular herbs used for treating PMS are chasteberry (for breast tenderness), ginkgo (for breast pain and emotional disturbance), evening primrose oil (for breast pain), dandelion (a natural diuretic used to reduce fluid retention

Coping with PMS (Premenstrual Syndrome)

and bloating), dong quai (for painful menstruation, lack or excess of bleeding, blood sugar stabilizing, bloating, sugar cravings, and cramps), and skullcap (for reducing nervous tension, tight muscles, headaches, cramps, and insomnia).

Most studies that have been conducted on these herbs have found them to be either ineffective or of only limited benefit in relieving PMS symptoms. Formal study of these herbs has been extremely limited, and there is simply not yet enough evidence available to say how safe or effective these natural remedies may be. Given this state of uncertainty, it is a good idea to discuss with your doctor in advance any herbal supplements you are thinking of taking.

Pain Medication

Medications of various kinds occasionally play a role in the treatment of troubling PMS symptoms. Medications have two names. The first is the generic (scientific) name; the second is the trade (commercial) name.

If headache, backache, or breast soreness are your major symptoms, the doctor may prescribe some type of pain medication. Prostaglandin inhibitors, such as aspirin and ibuprofen (Advil, Motrin, Nuprin) have anti-inflammatory and painkilling effects. Many health professionals believe ibuprofen is the most effective and simple painkiller for PMS symptoms. You may have to experiment to see what works best for you. Possible side effects of overuse of pain medications include stomach irritation and occasional stomach ulcers. Acetaminophen (Tylenol) is another mild painkiller. Slightly stronger are the nonsteroidal anti-inflammatory drugs (NSAIDs); examples are naproxen (Anaprox or Naprosyn) and mefenamic acid (Ponstel). These medications have an even greater tendency to cause stomach irritation. Tender

Do You Need More Help?

breasts may also respond to a nonpain medication, bromocriptine, or Parlodel. Even though most of these medications are available from a drugstore without a prescription, consult with your doctor before taking any drug.

Birth Control Pills

Some doctors believe that birth control pills are the first medication to try in treating PMS. Oral contraceptives will do one of three things: nothing, make symptoms worse, or improve your comfort level. There is no way to predict who will benefit. If you want to go this route, the best thing is to try oral contraceptives for several months to see what happens.

Presently, new and improved birth control pills are being tested that may be more effective for more women in alleviating PMS symptoms. In a 2001 study conducted by Dr. Candace Brown of the University of Tennessee in Memphis, 258 women, who for six months took a birth control pill that released steady amounts of estrogen and progestin, experienced a significant reduction of PMS symptoms. This new birth control pill, which will be marketed under the name Yasmin and is awaiting final FDA approval, is a powerful diuretic that helps to reduce water retention, bloating, and discomfort. The pill also blocks the male hormones that are thought to cause the mood swings associated with PMS. Although participants in this study were women who experienced mild to average PMS symptoms, it is hoped that this new birth control pill will also help women with severe PMS and premenstrual dysphoric disorder.

Progesterone

Progesterone is the most widely discussed and the most controversial treatment for PMS. In the past, some medical experts hoped that various progesterone preparations would turn out to be the standard treatment of PMS. Although some women with severe PMS report relief from progesterone, studies have not proven its overall effectiveness.

Diuretics

Diuretics are sometimes called water pills because they reduce swelling and bloating by drawing water from your system. Occasionally people abuse diuretics. They think they will lose weight when they take them. But diuretics can be dangerous because they deplete the body of potassium, which can lead to serious heart problems.

Doctors sometimes prescribe the diuretic spironolactone (Aldactone) or other diuretics for swelling and bloating, but this drug should never be used during pregnancy. If you are sexually active, you must use birth control without fail before trying this medication.

Antidepressants

Mood changes are rarely severe enough or long-term enough to warrant antidepressant medications. Nevertheless, some doctors prescribe tricyclic antidepressants, such as amitryptyline (Elavil), nortriptalyne (Pamelor), or the newer, selective serotonin reuptake inhibitors (SSRIs), such as paroxetine (Paxil), sertraline (Zoloft), or fluoxetine (Prozac) for relief of the mood fluctuations of PMS. These drugs treat mood disorders, such as depression, by increasing the levels of serotonin in your brain. Serotonin is a neurotransmitter that has a strong effect on your mood and emotions.

Antidepressants and SSRIs are also used to treat PMDD, the severe form of PMS. A 1995 study conducted by the Canadian Fluoxetine/Premenstrual Dysphoria Collaborative

Do You Need More Help?

Study Group has shown that fluoxetine, an SSRI, when prescribed in relatively low doses, can be an effective treatment for tension, irritability, and depression with minimal side effects. Zoloft was shown to improve the PMS symptoms (including mood swings, depression, anger, and relationship difficulties) of more than half of the women who took part in a 1998 study conducted by the University of Texas Southwestern Medical Center at Dallas. In 2000, the University of Pennsylvania Medical Center reported similar success with the SSRI venlafaxine (Effexor).

If mood-related disturbances (low energy, fatigue, too much or too little appetite, irritability, impulsivity, depression) are your main symptoms, you should know that women are ten times more likely than men to become depressed. Hormonal changes may account for some of this tendency to depression. According to *The New Our Bodies, Ourselves*, those who experience premenstrual depression are usually concerned with problems that have been there all along. Knowing this may help you ride out your depression until the premenstrual phase passes, or you may decide to get help in the form of counseling or a support group.

Antianxiety Agents

Anxiety can be a vague feeling of dread, or it can manifest itself as a difficulty in concentrating, excessive worry, restlessness, shortness of breath, heart palpitations, and panic attacks. Antianxiety medications are seldom necessary for mild to moderate PMS. Although they do seem to be useful for some women with severe PMS, they can also cause serious side effects, including addiction. Examples of these drugs are diazepam (Valium) and alprazolam (Xanax). Some physicians taper down the doses to avoid dependency.

Coping with PMS (Premenstrual Syndrome)

Antidepressants and SSRIs may relieve such symptoms as anxiety, impulsiveness, aggression, and increased appetite, but they are not at all helpful in alleviating the physical symptoms of PMS. If you have mild to moderate PMS, you should not consider taking these medications. Instead of chemicals, use the relaxation techniques you learned in the last chapter to rid your body and mind of stress and anxiety.

Acupuncture

Acupuncture is a part of Chinese medicine that involves using fine needles to regulate the flow of energy (called chi) in the body and to remove blockages to this energy flow. The application of heat and massage may also be part of the process. Those who advocate acupuncture for PMS consider the condition an imbalance in the body's vital energy.

Acupressure

Acupressure can be a part of an acupuncture procedure or can be performed alone. Instead of using needles to change the energy flow of the body, the practitioner applies pressure to various body points. Shiatsu is one of the many other forms of acupuncture.

Homeopathy

Homeopathic medicine uses natural substances to cure a variety of medical problems. Oil of evening primrose, a commonly prescribed treatment for premenstrual breast soreness, fits into this category of remedies. Evening primrose is a common wildflower of North America. Its oil contains the essential fatty acid gamma-linolenic acid. Some people say this preparation has helped reduce other PMS symptoms, such as mood swings. If you are interested in

Do You Need More Help?

trying homeopathy, go to a respected, knowledgeable practitioner rather than trying to treat yourself.

Reflexology
According to this method of healing, pressing on various places on your feet or hands will correct imbalances in various parts of your body. The concept may sound strange to you, but some women swear it brings relief.

Therapeutic Touch
Therapeutic touch is an ancient healing art that has recently been rediscovered by Western practitioners. This healing method may sound the strangest of all, but many professionals endorse it. Rather than touching the body as the name implies, the practitioner uses the energy field surrounding the patient to affect bodily changes. Practitioners teach techniques to relieve stress, to decrease chronic pain, and to increase energy.

A Look at the Big Picture

PMS experts have made the following overall observations about PMS and its treatment.

PMS is tenacious. You have to be strong as you struggle with it. Linda's PMS began in her first year of college. She says, "PMS has taken a terrific toll on me and my family. I feel like I've tried hundreds of different remedies. In spite of that, I've often spent an entire day in bed. My husband's favorite line is, 'Why don't you do something about it?' He's an engineer who's used to solving problems. He can't seem to understand that treating PMS isn't as straightforward. But he's trying his best to be patient and supportive."

Coping with PMS (Premenstrual Syndrome)

If you are susceptible, PMS may never completely disappear. It may go away for a while, only to reappear later. Linda adds, "I never give up hope that one day my PMS will completely disappear. Several months ago for no reason, my periods stopped for a couple of months. Since that time, I've still had PMS, but it's much less severe. PMS is something I know I'll have to accept as a part of my life."

Remedies that work for your friend may not work for you. It may be frustrating, but try not to let it discourage you from seeking out other remedies. "I had a friend who swore by large doses of vitamins and fish oil," Linda says. "I took vitamins for a while. If anything, they made me feel worse."

At work Linda tried to keep quiet about her PMS. But her silence and obvious distress made her coworkers nervous. They wanted to help but didn't know what to do. One day Karen started talking about her PMS. After this sharing period, Linda told Karen her story. United in their struggle, the two became friends. Sharing made Linda's discomfort bearable, and her coworkers didn't feel awkward around her anymore.

Medical doctors most often support the lifestyle changes discussed in chapter 4. In the rare case in which PMS turns a person's life upside down and medical intervention seems necessary, a doctor may try various medications and offer reassurance that nothing more serious is going on.

Self-Help, Psychotherapy, and Support Groups

We've already discussed lifestyle changes as a form of self-help. But there is more you can do to help yourself.

Dealing with Friends and Family

If you are reading this book, you are already helping yourself or someone else get a handle on PMS. You have learned one thing about the condition: It comes in cycles. Don't assume that the problems and symptoms will go away forever after one particularly bad menstrual cycle. Chances are they will return. Therefore it is a good idea to talk to your friends and family about it. Don't keep PMS information a secret. One way you can help others is to share what you know.

If you are still living at home, you may need to point out to brothers, sisters, and your parents what a nice person you are to live with most of the time. Ask if they will cut you some slack during PMS time.

Planning Around PMS

If physical discomfort and mood problems affect you premenstrually, you may find advance planning helpful. PMS comes around every month with annoying regularity. Why not plan for it? Here are a few things you can do:

Coping with PMS (Premenstrual Syndrome)

↪ Schedule fewer activities (perhaps only the necessary ones) on the days you suspect symptoms will be most severe. Make yourself less busy, and plan to devote more time to pampering yourself or doing whatever you need to do to gain control: A bubble bath? Exercise? Spending more time alone?

↪ In order to do less on PMS days, you may have to accomplish more during the rest of your cycle.

↪ Figure out what you will want or need on PMS days. Tell your family about your plan to post a list somewhere, such as on the refrigerator, for all to see. Here is Celeste's list. "Today I would like to: (1) Go with Lonnie to work out at the gym, (2) Make my own dinner when I get home, (3) Do my job (dishes) when I'm done with dinner, and (4) Do my homework after that." Celeste's family (her younger sister, two older brothers, her mother and father) took to this list posting with ease. Then they knew exactly what to expect.

Accept Support

The advice to accept support may seem unnecessary at best and silly at worst, but it can't hurt you to hear it anyway. It is not someone else's responsibility to remember to give you support. You may have to ask. Even though PMS may feel just as bad, it is not an obvious and visible condition like an infected finger or a broken leg.

As strange as it seems, you may have fallen into the habit of going it alone. Says Stephanie, "People just don't understand. How could they? Especially my boyfriend. He doesn't have PMS."

Self-Help, Psychotherapy, and Support Groups

What Stephanie says is true. Only you can feel what you are feeling. But people who love you do want to help. They probably do not know what to do. You may need to tell them.

"But I don't know what to tell them," Stephanie says. "How can they understand when I don't know myself?"

What Stephanie needs to say, though it will not be easy, is that she does not know exactly what she needs. She may have to tell her boyfriend that she values his support and expressions of caring, and that during her PMS she needs him to show her these even more.

Dealing with Anger and Depression

Managing anger is a job for everyone, not just for those with PMS. Everyone gets mad; some people feel angry several times a day. Others carry their anger around like a purse full of stones. Someone who says, "I never get angry," may be ignoring his or her feelings and may have trouble recognizing his or her own anger.

Anger is not a bad emotion. In fact, anger can be very useful. Feelings of outrage are often catalysts for accomplishing important tasks. For example, anger at overflowing landfills fueled the recycling effort. Anger over the unjust treatment of African Americans started the civil rights movement.

Turning anger inward and causing depression is unhealthy, but so is letting it explode. In *The Dance of Anger: A Woman's Guide to Changing the Patterns of Intimate Relationships*, Harriet Goldhor Lerner, Ph.D., states that venting our anger does no good unless we also change our unhealthy ways of relating to others. She identifies two common behavior patterns in women: the "nice

Coping with PMS (Premenstrual Syndrome)

lady" and the "bitch." Both reinforce old stereotypes and keep women confined within a narrow range of expression. "Nice ladies" are afraid to express anger even when an expression of true feelings is justified. These women's anger eventually explodes at inappropriate times, and they end up feeling guilty. A "bitchy" woman may spend her energy trying (unsuccessfully) to change another person instead of focusing on herself. Both ways of relating make women feel powerless and lead to further anger.

Psychologist Susan Heitler, in the *Rocky Mountain News*, October 23, 1996, said that people who are depressed have aimed their anger inward and usually feel mad at themselves. They are actually mad at someone (or something) that has taken away their control. If we apply this theory to PMS, it is no wonder that people become furious and depressed over a condition that seems to have a will of its own. Obviously, the only way to conquer PMS is to gain control over it. If you have a temper tantrum or go into a rage, your anger is in control of the situation, not you.

The Institute for Mental Health Initiatives suggests that when you start to get angry, you consider one word: RETHINK.

R stands for recognize. Recognize and acknowledge your anger.

E stands for empathize. The dictionary defines empathy as "understanding so intimate that the feelings, thoughts, and motives of one are readily comprehended by another." In other words, trying to understand where another person is coming from. This can be hard when you're steaming mad, but give it a try.

Self-Help, Psychotherapy, and Support Groups

T stands for think. Think about the anger-producing incident in a new and different way. Can you see humor in the situation? Did you have a part in the problem? Do you have any ideas for solving it?

H stands for hear. Hear what the other person has to say. Really listen. Repeat back what you think you heard.

I stands for integrate. Integrate love and respect. Use "I" messages to state your opinion on how what happened makes you feel. "I" messages are statements about how you feel as opposed to statements condemning another's behavior. For example, "I feel discounted when someone doesn't listen to me." Another: "I feel angry when I am interrupted." Notice what works in controlling your anger. Exercise, journal keeping, hot baths, hugs?

N stands for notice. Notice what works to control your anger.

K stands for keep your focus. Keep your focus on the present. Don't rehash old hurts or bring up grudges.

Let's see how the RETHINK method might play out in actual practice.

The Scene: You are definitely in your PMS phase. Your hands and feet are swollen, your head is pounding, and your lower abdominal area feels like it has been punched. As a way of gaining control, you decide to wear your favorite shirt, the one you ironed two days ago. You look for it in the closet; it's not there.

Of course, your sister has it. She always borrows your clothes without asking. But she knows it is your favorite

Coping with PMS (Premenstrual Syndrome)

shirt, and she saw you ironing it. How could she? You want to strangle her, but she has already gone to school. What can you do? You would like to rip her clothes to shreds.

But wait. You have written RETHINK across your bedroom mirror. You are willing to try this new method.

Recognize your anger. No problem. You're furious!

Empathize. See the situation from her viewpoint. Well, you have borrowed her clothes at times.

Think about the situation in a new way. Maybe you could ask her if you could wear her new dress for your date this weekend.

Hear what she says. She isn't here now, but you will see her at school. She had better have a good reason.

Integrate respect and love. You do love her. You have had a lot of fun times together. And she is your only sister.

Notice what works to control your anger. It would probably help to write her a note. It always makes you feel better to express your feelings in writing.

Keep your attention on the present. You have to. You do not have time to bring up all the other times your sister has borrowed your clothes. You have more important things to do.

If RETHINK is too hard to remember, here's something easier to use when you get angry. Think of a traffic light, red, yellow, and green:

Self-Help, Psychotherapy, and Support Groups

Red: Stop. Don't react. Isolate yourself, if necessary.

Yellow: Take some time, maybe until the end of your PMS.

Green: Find the person with whom you've disagreed. Talk things over.

Helpers: Counselors and Therapists

If you have severe mood swings or depression, or if you feel you cannot relieve your stress alone, you may decide to talk with a counselor.

You do not have to have a major mood disorder to benefit from seeing a counselor. Almost everyone can use this kind of support from time to time. Sometimes because of attitudes within their families, young women feel ashamed or embarrassed to take this step ("I'm not crazy. Why should I see a therapist?") Look at it this way: If you had strep throat, would you refuse to take penicillin? If you had an infected toe, would you avoid medical treatment?

Because there are so many types of helpers with so many different attitudes and abilities, you cannot be too careful in choosing one. Depending on where you live, your mode of transportation, your health insurance, and your finances, you may not have much choice. However, you always have the choice to stop therapy if the therapist you have chosen is not helpful. States differ in the ways they regulate mental-health professionals. Therapist, counselor, and psychotherapist are generic terms that anyone can use. People who put these titles after their names may or may not be certified or licensed to practice psychotherapy in your state.

Coping with PMS (Premenstrual Syndrome)

A certified therapist has completed specialized training and should have a certificate to prove it. Angie's mother had a master's degree in nursing and for many years taught at the college level. She attended a part-time program in family therapy for two years and received her certificate. Although she is now a certified therapist, she would need to spend many more hours in supervised practice in order to become a licensed marriage and family therapist.

A licensed therapist, such as a licensed clinical social worker, has met various requirements for practicing in the state and has passed an examination by the state board of examiners. This person may use initials, such as LCSW (for licensed clinical social worker), after his or her name.

Usually, professionals such as psychiatrists, psychiatric nurses, psychologists, and social workers are regulated by a state board. If you have questions about a therapist's license or other questions about qualifications, ask the therapist or call the appropriate state board. You should be able to find a listing in the telephone directory. Just as you have rights as a consumer of medical services, you have rights as a consumer of mental-health services. It is extremely important to feel comfortable with a mental-health worker. The National Organization for Women (NOW) has developed a Bill of Rights for the consumer of psychotherapy. The following questions are adapted from it. Your first right, which is the foundation for all the rest, is the right to ask questions, such as:

Self-Help, Psychotherapy, and Support Groups

1. How do you feel about women and their special circumstances?

2. What is your training, what are your qualifications, how long have you done this work, and how much experience have you had with emotional problems related to PMS?

3. What are your appointment policies and procedures? (For example, many mental-health professionals charge for an appointment that is not canceled twenty-four hours in advance.)

4. What are your fees, and will my health insurance cover any or all of the costs?

5. Is what I say to you confidential?

6. What is your policy regarding the termination of therapy?

Most mental-health practitioners disclose this type of information on the first visit. Some offer you an informational visit without charge.

Types of Mental-Health Professionals

Not all counselors have degrees in psychology or are trained in the field of mental health. Pastoral counselors are priests, ministers, or laypersons from particular religious traditions who have hands-on experience with the real-life troubles, stresses, and worries of their congregations.

Coping with PMS (Premenstrual Syndrome)

Those with undergraduate degrees in social work can put the initials BSW after their names. They may be called social workers. Those with a master's degree in social work use the initials MSW. If they have had a required number of supervised hours in clinical settings and have passed state licensing exams, they can use the initials LCSW (or similar initials).

Although some with a master's degree call themselves psychologists, clinical psychologists should have a doctorate (Ph.D. or Psy.D.), supervised hours of practice, and a license to practice in their state. Ph.D. and Psy.D. psychologists are not medical doctors and cannot prescribe medications.

Psychiatrists are medical doctors with specialized training in psychiatry, the science of mental disorders. A psychiatrist has had four years of medical school training after college plus several years of specialized training in psychiatry. A psychiatrist may be the specialist who prescribes and monitors medications for anxiety and depression. You may have a psychiatrist as your primary mental-health counselor, or he or she may be an occasional consultant. Fees for psychiatrists are usually higher than those for other therapists.

Family therapists may have their basic training in pastoral counseling, social work, psychology, or psychiatry. They have further training in dealing with people as members of family groups. In therapy, they often bring in other family members and emphasize the influence of the family (perhaps stretching back several generations) on the client.

When you are choosing a therapist, the main thing to evaluate is how that person works with you. Are you comfortable with the person? Do you feel better after your sessions? (Sometimes people don't feel good after a session but believe they have made progress in problem solving or working on difficult issues in their lives.)

Self-Help, Psychotherapy, and Support Groups

Support Groups

Informal Support Groups
Support groups don't have to be large; you and one other person can make up a group of two. In fact, the person most often mentioned as a support by the young women interviewed was mom. Mom's help ranged from explaining about menstruation to giving advice on pain medications.

Formal Support Groups
A formal support group may be hard to find. If you live in a big city, you may be able to locate one through a university medical center or a PMS clinic. If you are seeing a physician or an alternative medical person, be sure to ask for a referral to a group. A support group may be a supplement to medical treatment or may be a person's main resource for help. Sometimes in the absence of a PMS group, young women find support at a twelve-step program, such as Al-Anon or Overeaters Anonymous. The problem is not the same, but the coping mechanisms may be similar (and be sure to check the resources listed at the end of this book). If you can't find a support group, you may want to start one yourself. If you can get two or three people together on a regular basis, you have your group. Be sure to keep the discussion upbeat, focusing on remedies that have helped. If you find someone to talk to on the Internet, be sure to remember that what you are learning may be only one person's opinion and not a treatment that has been scientifically tested.

Finally, try reading some of the latest reports on research into the causes and treatment of PMS. These days scientists are not only taking premenstrual syndrome seriously but are testing new and better ways of treating it.

Coping with PMS (Premenstrual Syndrome)

Advice for Family and Friends

If you are a family member or a friend of a young woman with PMS, you have probably felt as helpless as the person with the symptoms. Maybe you have felt even more helpless. At least the affected person can do something—exercise, make dietary changes, get more sleep, see a therapist. What can you do?

The most important thing for you to do is be a source of support for the other person. Someone with PMS can often feel alone and emotionally isolated. Start by being a listener. For most of us, active listening is a hard job. We want to do the talking. But when its PMS time for your daughter, sister, or friend, try to tune in to her words and her feelings. Open-ended comments such as "I bet you get tired of going through this every month" may elicit a "yes," more feelings, and the comment that you are very understanding. Sometimes your friend or family member doesn't want advice; she just wants to talk.

Healthy Recipes for Busy Young Women

Because healthful eating is such an important part of PMS control, let's talk about a lifelong plan.

Proteins, Carbohydrates, and Fats

Nutritionists divide foods into these categories: proteins, carbohydrates, fats, vitamins, and minerals.

Proteins, made up of smaller units called amino acids, are important in the making of hormones, muscle tissue, and enzymes.

Carbohydrates are either simple or complex. Sugar is a simple carbohydrate. Complex carbohydrates are made up of chains of sugars. A generation ago, people thought that eating complex carbohydrates, such as potatoes and pasta, would make them overweight. Experts now understand that this is not true and advise the consumption of more complex carbohydrates.

Fats are classified as saturated or unsaturated. Experts advise avoiding an overload of all fats, but especially of saturated fats. These are the ones that make people more prone to heart disease. The nutrition labels on all packaged foods will tell you how much saturated and unsaturated fat are in the food products.

Coping with PMS (Premenstrual Syndrome)

Vitamins and minerals assist with various body functions and occur naturally in the food groups recommended below. Other than a daily multivitamin, which some doctors suggest, vitamin supplements may not be necessary and can be dangerous in large doses.

The U.S. Department of Agriculture and the U.S. Department of Health and Human Services regularly publish dietary guidelines for Americans to help you make responsible food choices. The Food Guide Pyramid, which you may have seen on bread wrappers or cereal boxes, includes five major food groups that serve as the basis for everyday good eating. The largest sections (the ones nearest the bottom of the pyramid) include foods we need to eat the most. These foods come from plants.

At the bottom of the pyramid is the grain products group. This group includes cold cereals, hot cereals, bread, rice, noodles, and grains. Choose nine to eleven servings a day from this group.

Sharing the next level of the pyramid are the vegetable group (three to five servings) and the fruit group (two to four servings a day).

Next comes the dairy group (milk, yogurt, and cheese). Adults do well with two to three servings a day from this group, but young people between the ages of eleven and twenty-four should have five servings per day. During adolescence, the bones grow fast and have an increased need for the calcium in the dairy group and in some fortified foods. On the same level is the meat and beans group (lean meat, poultry, fish, dry beans, eggs, and nuts), two to three servings a day.

At the very top of the food pyramid, to be used sparingly, are fats, oils, and sweets.

Healthy Recipes for Busy Young Women

How many servings do you need? Almost everyone should eat at least the minimum number from each food group. What is a serving? Good question. One serving in the grain products group is a slice of bread (make that whole wheat) or a bowl of cereal (three-fourths of a cup). A whole sandwich for lunch would count as two servings of grain. A cup of spaghetti for dinner counts as two servings.

A serving of fruit is any piece of fresh fruit (apple, orange, banana), a half-cup of canned fruit, or three-quarters of a cup of fruit juice. For one serving in the vegetable category, eat a cup of leafy green lettuce, one-half a cup of cooked or chopped raw vegetables, or three-quarters of a cup of vegetable juice.

If you are under twenty-five years of age, you should drink three glasses of skim milk a day (or you can substitute low-fat yogurt for some of the milk). Another food in the milk group is cheese (one and a half ounces of natural cheese or two ounces of processed cheese).

In the meat and beans group, try two ounces of lean meat, poultry, or fish. An egg, two tablespoons of peanut butter, or one-third of a cup of nuts counts as an ounce of meat.

Some foods fit into more than one group. For example, you can count dry beans and peas as meat servings or as vegetable servings. An example given in a colorful chart published by the Education Department of the National Livestock and Meat Board cites a large slice of sausage pizza as having ingredients in four food groups: crust (grain products group), tomato sauce (vegetable group), cheese (milk group), and sausage (meat and beans group). The pizza also contains a portion of your daily fat intake.

Coping with PMS (Premenstrual Syndrome)

Put On Your Apron

You may not be the major cook in your family. And when it is PMS time, the last thing you want to do is sweat over a hot stove. But once in a while, you may want to amaze your family with a well-balanced dinner—your kind of dinner. Or maybe you would like a few recipes for quick-and-easy snack foods.

Remember, your goal is to incorporate nutritious foods all month. Healthy eating will then become a pattern for you.

Many of the following sample recipes were submitted by high school and college-age women who like to cook for themselves and/or their families. Most are quick and made with readily available, PMS-fighting ingredients. You will not find any recipes with thirty or forty ingredients; most have fewer than ten things to combine. Servings may be for one person but can also be enough for two, four, or six persons. If you get into the cooking mood, you may want to invest in one or two of the many health-food cookbooks available at supermarkets and bookstores. Three of the many magazines that offer tips for healthy eating are *Cooking Light, The Nutrition Action Health Letter*, and *Prevention*.

Let's start with the grain products group: cereals, rice, pasta, and bread.

Grains

Nutrition experts recommend eating healthy breakfasts, and grains are a great way to start the day. If you are tired of the same old cornflakes, try adding a couple of

Healthy Recipes for Busy Young Women

tablespoons of dried fruits to your cereal. These days, the variety available is nothing short of amazing: raisins, cherries, pineapple, dates, figs, mangos, papayas. In season, you can add all kinds of berries.

If you prefer hot cereal, you can add the same dried fruits during cooking. Also try substituting apple juice for some or all of the liquid used in cooking.

Here is a fun way to eat cereal. You could even make a few batches of Aunt Gertie's Granola for your friends.

Aunt Gertie's Granola
   2 cups quick-cooking (but not instant) rolled oats
   1 cup chopped, unsalted, dry-roasted, shelled peanuts
   1/4 cup wheat germ
   1/4 cup honey
   1/4 cup apple juice
   1/2 cup chopped walnuts or pecans
   1 tablespoon canola oil
   1/2 cup dried fruit (optional)

In a large bowl, combine oats, wheat germ, and nuts. Combine the honey, apple juice, and oil in another bowl. Add the second mixture to the first. Spread in a jelly-roll pan or on a cookie sheet. Bake at 300°F for 30 to 40 minutes or until mixture turns light brown. Stir every 15 minutes. Remove from oven and transfer to a cool pan. Break up into chunks. Stir in dried fruit, if desired (this addition tends to make your crunchy granola less crunchy). Store it in containers with tight lids, or put it into plastic bags to give to your friends. They'll love it, and they'll love you, too.

Coping with PMS (Premenstrual Syndrome)

Breakfast Bulghur

If you are looking for something different for breakfast, something heartier, try cracked-wheat bulghur.

- 1/2 cup bulghur
- 1 cup water
- 1/4 teaspoon salt (optional)
- 1 teaspoon low-sugar preserves or fruit-only preserves (optional)
- Skim milk (optional)

Combine bulghur and water. Bring to a boil, then reduce heat and simmer in a covered saucepan for 10 to 12 minutes until bulghur is tender and water is absorbed. Serve with low-sugar preserves and/or skim milk.

Antoinette's Easy French Toast for Two

This is another simple dish you can eat anytime. Antoinette and her mother like to make it for Sunday brunch. Using egg product is considered healthier because it eliminates the cholesterol from egg yolks.

- 1/4 cup egg product or two eggs, separated and beaten
- 1/4 cup skim milk
- 1/4 cup orange juice
- 4 slices somewhat stale bread, preferably whole wheat
- 1 or 2 teaspoons canola oil (or enough to keep toast from sticking)

Healthy Recipes for Busy Young Women

In a shallow bowl, mix the eggs, milk, and juice. Place each slice of bread into the mixture for 5 seconds. Let the bread soak up the egg for 5 seconds on the other side. Brush a large nonstick skillet with half the oil. Lay two of the egg-covered slices in the skillet, and cook them on medium heat. Then two more with the remaining oil. Serve with low-sugar syrup. Like many recipes, this recipe has elements of more than one food group.

Wonderful Wheat Pancakes
    1 cup whole-wheat flour
    1/4 cup unbleached flour
    2 tablespoons wheat germ
    1 tablespoon brown sugar
    1 teaspoon baking powder
    1/4 teaspoon baking soda
    1/4 teaspoon salt
    1 egg, beaten, or 1/4 cup egg product
    1 1/4 cups low-fat buttermilk
    1 tablespoon canola oil

In a medium-sized bowl, combine dry ingredients. Combine liquids, except oil, in another bowl. Add liquid ingredients to dry mixture and blend. Use a small amount of the oil on a griddle or frying pan. When the griddle is hot, add 1/4 cup of batter for each pancake. Turn pancakes when surface bubbles. Cook pancakes in this manner until all of the batter is used up. Serve with fresh fruit. Makes about 8 pancakes.

Coping with PMS (Premenstrual Syndrome)

Easy Couscous Soup for One or Two
Whether this serves one or two depends on how much you like it and also on how many other things you are having for lunch or dinner.

- 1 medium onion, chopped
- 2 medium tomatoes, chopped
- 2 cloves garlic, peeled and minced
- 1 can vegetable broth
- 1 cup couscous, precooked according to package directions
- Salt and pepper to taste
- 2 tablespoons Parmesan cheese

Sauté onion, tomatoes, and garlic in a small amount of olive oil. Add vegetable broth and couscous. Bring to boiling point and simmer, but do not boil. Serve with Parmesan cheese.

Wild-ish Rice
Because it is hard to grow (and it mainly grows on its own in a limited area), wild rice is an expensive item. With this recipe you can fool your guests and make believe you are living on the "wild side."

- 1 cup regular uncooked rice (not the instant kind)
- 2 tablespoons margarine
- 1 small can (4 ounces) undrained mushrooms, sliced
- 1/4 teaspoon thyme
- 1 can consommé
- 1 can water (use the consommé can)
- 1/4 teaspoon rosemary
- Nonstick vegetable spray

Healthy Recipes for Busy Young Women

Spray a 9-inch by 13-inch baking dish with nonstick spray. Pour in all ingredients. Cover loosely with foil. Bake at 350°F for about an hour until liquid is absorbed and rice is tender. Stir once at about 30 minutes. Serves 4 to 6.

Chickpea Sauce and Spaghetti

You don't need to add salt to this recipe because the canned chickpeas (garbanzo beans) and Parmesan cheese make it salty enough.

- 2 15-ounce cans chickpeas, undrained
- 2 tablespoons vegetable oil, preferably olive
- 4 large cloves garlic, minced (4 teaspoons)
- 1 1/2 large onions, thinly sliced
- 1 16-ounce can tomatoes, drained and cut up with the liquid reserved
- 1 teaspoon rosemary, crushed
- 1/4 cup minced fresh parsley
- Freshly ground black pepper to taste
- 1 pound spaghetti, cooked and drained
- 1/4 cup grated Parmesan cheese

In a blender, food processor, or sieve, puree 1 can of chickpeas with liquid. In a large saucepan, heat the oil and sauté the garlic and onion until garlic begins to brown. Add the tomatoes and their liquid, rosemary, chickpea puree, and the remaining can of chickpeas with liquid to the saucepan. Stirring often, heat the mixture for about 15 minutes or until it has thickened. Add parsley and pepper. Toss the hot cooked spaghetti with the sauce and sprinkle with Parmesan before serving. Serves 6.

Coping with PMS (Premenstrual Syndrome)

Szechuan Noodles with Peanut Sauce

You only have to cook the pasta for this easy-to-prepare dish. Serve it hot or at room temperature.

    12 ounces spaghetti, linguine, or similar pasta
    1/3 cup hot water
    1/3 cup smooth peanut butter (preferably all-natural)
    2 teaspoons reduced-sodium soy sauce
    2 teaspoons vinegar
    2 scallions, finely chopped, divided (set aside 1 tablespoon to use as a garnish)
    2 cloves garlic, finely minced
    1 teaspoon sugar
    1/4 hot red pepper flakes, or more, to taste

Cook the pasta in boiling water until it's firm. Drain it, set it aside, and keep it warm. While the pasta cooks, make the sauce. In a medium bowl, blend water and peanut butter. Stir in soy sauce, vinegar, scallions, garlic, sugar, and hot pepper flakes. Garnish with reserved scallions. Combine the sauce with hot spaghetti in a heated serving dish. Serves 4.

Fettuccini with Fresh Herbs

This pasta recipe comes from Susan Stevens, author of *Delitefully Healthmark . . . Cooking for the Health of It.*

    4 ounces eggless fettuccini
    1 clove garlic, minced

Healthy Recipes for Busy Young Women

1 tablespoon olive oil
1/4 cup chopped parsley
1/3 cup chopped fresh basil
2 tomatoes, chopped
Fresh-ground black pepper

Cook pasta according to package directions, omitting salt. Drain. In a saucepan, sauté garlic in olive oil until golden. Add pasta, herbs, and chopped tomatoes. Season to taste with black pepper. Serves 4 as a side dish.

Two-Way Potatoes (Sometimes called Twice-Baked Potatoes)

This is an old favorite for those who like their potatoes two ways—baked and mashed.

2 large baking potatoes
Skim milk, warmed
Salt and pepper to taste

Scrub the potatoes, poke each one many times with a fork, and bake them for about an hour in an oven preheated to 325°F. Cut each potato in half lengthwise. Cool potato halves until you can handle them. Scoop out fleshy part of potato, leaving a rim of about 1/4 inch. Mash potato pulp and add enough warm milk to make the potatoes creamy. Beat with a whisk. Season with salt and pepper. Spoon the potato mixture back into skins. Broil until lightly brown on top (about 5 minutes).

Coping with PMS (Premenstrual Syndrome)

Fruits and Vegetables

Now that you have climbed to the second level of the food pyramid, greet two categories of foods that need little or no preparation for eating.

Smoothies

Smoothie, citrus slush, fruit shake—these are all varieties of delicious, easy-to-make fruit drinks. The following recipe will give you an idea of what you can do with some fruit and a blender. (You'll find more smoothie recipes in the yogurt/milk section.)

O.B. (Orange Banana) Shake
    1 cup skim milk
    1 ripe banana
    1/4 cup frozen orange juice concentrate

Mix all in blender and drink.

Fruit Kabobs

If you (or someone you know) will not eat fruit, here is a way to increase your (or his or her) interest. Buy a package of wooden skewers, available in most supermarkets. Cut fruits into 1-inch squares. (Most fruits, except citrus fruits and melons, will need a squirt of lemon juice to prevent discoloration after being cut or peeled.) Thread on skewers alternate chunks of pineapple, cantaloupe, honeydew melon, watermelon, peaches, nectarines, apricots, bananas, and grapes. Serve before dinner as a colorful appetizer.

Healthy Recipes for Busy Young Women

My Granny's Marinated Vegetable Salad
   1 cup fresh broccoli tops (florets)
   1 cup carrots, sliced diagonally
   1 cup cauliflowerettes
   1 cup celery, sliced diagonally
   1/2 cup green or red pepper strips
   1/2 cup green onions, chopped
   1 cup apple juice, unsweetened
   1/2 cup cider vinegar
   3/4 teaspoon black pepper

In a small amount of water, steam (for 3 or 4 minutes) the first four vegetables until barely tender. Cool. In a large bowl, combine steamed vegetables with peppers and onions. In a separate bowl, mix the apple juice, vinegar, and pepper. Stir the mixture and cover it. Refrigerate the vegetables overnight.

Nellie's Veggies
   1/2 pound fresh broccoli, washed and trimmed
   1/2 pound fresh cauliflower, washed and trimmed
   4 or 5 cloves garlic, peeled and chopped fine
   2 tablespoons low-sodium soy sauce
   2 tablespoons olive oil

Place broccoli and cauliflower on a broiler pan or cookie sheet. Mix the last 3 ingredients and drizzle on the veggies. Put the pan on the top oven rack and bake at 450°F until the veggies are crispy and lightly browned. Check them often; at this temperature, they can burn quickly.

Billy Goat Gruff Greens
    1/2 head romaine lettuce, washed and dried
    3/4 cup fresh, shredded Parmesan cheese
    1/4 cup Caesar dressing diluted with vinegar

In a large bowl, break up the lettuce leaves into bite-sized pieces. Sprinkle with cheese. Just before serving, drizzle dressing over greens. Toss and eat. If you don't mind limp lettuce, the greens will still taste good the next day.

Erica's Colorful Cabbage
    1/2 pound cabbage, shredded or sliced in fine strips
    1/2 cup carrots, shredded
    1/2 cup broccoli florets and stems, chopped
    1/2 cup cherry tomatoes, quartered
    1/2 cup celery, sliced
    1/2 cup fresh parsley, chopped
    1/4 cup canola oil
    2 tablespoons cider vinegar
    1 tablespoon Dijon mustard
    1/2 teaspoon salt
    1/2 teaspoon pepper

In large bowl, combine cabbage, carrots, broccoli, tomatoes, and celery. Put the rest of the ingredients in a tightly covered jar and shake well. Pour over the cabbage mixture.

Oven Stew
This stew contains meat, but it fits here in the vegetable category because it contains onion, celery, carrots, and green beans (optional). This winter recipe cooks all by itself in the oven while you warm yourself by the fireplace.

Healthy Recipes for Busy Young Women

- 1 pound lean beef, such as bottom round steak, cut into 1/2-inch cubes
- 2 medium red potatoes cut into small pieces (just scrub them—no need to peel)
- 1 medium onion, chopped
- 4 stalks celery, sliced
- 3 large carrots, sliced
- 1/2 pound fresh green beans (optional)
- 1 cup tomato juice
- 1 tablespoon sugar
- 1/2 teaspoon salt
- 1/2 teaspoon black pepper
- 1/2 teaspoon basil

Combine all the ingredients except potatoes in a 2 1/2 quart, ovenproof, covered casserole dish or Dutch oven. Bake at 325°F for 3 hours. Stir several times during baking. Add water, if necessary. Stir in potatoes during last hour. Serves 6.

Meat, Poultry, Fish, Dry Beans and Peas, Eggs, and Nuts

Climbing up the pyramid, you will come next to this large group, which provides many choices for the two to three servings you need each day.

Spicy Chicken

- 1/4 teaspoon garlic powder
- 2 teaspoons ground cumin
- 2 teaspoons chili powder
- 1/4 teaspoon salt

Coping with PMS (Premenstrual Syndrome)

    1/2 teaspoon black pepper
    1 teaspoon sugar
    3 tablespoons Worcestershire sauce
    1 pound boneless, skinless chicken breasts
    Nonstick vegetable spray

Mix the first seven ingredients. Spray a 9-inch by 13-inch glass dish with nonstick spray. Place the chicken pieces in the dish and pour liquid mixture over them. Cover lightly with foil. Bake at 350°F for 40 minutes or until the chicken is done.

Simple Salmon (on the grill)
    32-ounces of salmon fillets
    Olive or canola oil
    Salt and pepper to taste
    Lemon wedges

Make sure the grill is clean; brush with oil. Use medium heat. Brush the fillets on both sides with oil. Sprinkle them with salt and pepper. Grill them for about 5 or 10 minutes on each side, depending on the thickness of the fillets. The fish is done when the center of the fillet turns light pink. Serves 4.

Chicken in Currant Sauce
This recipe is very simple, delicious, and impressive. Your relatives will think you can really cook. You can.

    About 1 pound boneless, skinless chicken breasts
    1 medium onion, sliced

Healthy Recipes for Busy Young Women

1/2 cup water
1/4 cup currant jelly or preserves
1 tablespoon Dijon mustard

Put all the ingredients in a large skillet. Bring the liquid mixture to a boil, reduce heat, and simmer for 25 to 30 minutes or until done. During cooking, turn the breasts at least once. Watch carefully; if the liquid evaporates, add a little water. (This recipe is from the American Institute for Cancer Research.)

Marinated Garbanzos
1 can chickpeas, drained and rinsed with cold water
Basic Dressing #1 (see recipe at end of this chapter), or use a bottled Italian dressing

Pour a small amount of dressing over the chickpeas; marinate the mixture for several hours. Add to a green salad at serving time.

Baked Garbanzos
1 can chickpeas, drained
1 teaspoon olive oil

Toss the chickpeas with the oil. Bake for an hour (stirring occasionally) at 350°F. Eat as a snack or use in salads. Store in refrigerator; they don't stay fresh forever. You now have on hand a good source of fiber, B_6, iron, and magnesium. (This recipe is compliments of *Prevention*, November 1996.)

Coping with PMS (Premenstrual Syndrome)

Mexican Bean Salad
- 1 16-ounce can black beans, drained
- 1 cup canned corn, drained
- 1/2 cup Italian dressing or 1/4 cup Basic Dressing #1 (see recipe at end of chapter)
- 4 ounces cheddar cheese
- 2 fresh tomatoes, quartered
- 4 cups washed and dried romaine or leaf lettuce, torn into small pieces

Mix the beans and the corn with the dressing. Marinate for at least an hour. Divide the lettuce onto four salad plates. Spoon the corn and bean mixture over the lettuce. Sprinkle cheese on top. Decorate with tomatoes.

Split Pea with Mushroom Soup
This recipe uses green or yellow split peas, which usually need soaking. If you cook the soup long enough, however, they will soften on their own.

- 1 tablespoon canola oil
- 1 medium onion, chopped
- 2 cloves garlic, peeled and minced
- 3/4 cup yellow or green split peas
- 1 cup sliced mushrooms
- 1 medium carrot, peeled and chopped or 10 baby carrots, cut into small pieces
- 1 cup low-salt chicken broth
- 1/2 teaspoon black pepper
- Salt to taste

Healthy Recipes for Busy Young Women

Rinse the peas in a colander. In a large saucepan, sauté the onion, garlic, celery, carrots, and mushrooms until they have softened. Add the chicken broth and the split peas. Reduce heat, cover, and simmer soup for 45 minutes or until the peas are soft. Stir occasionally. At this point, you can eat the soup and see all the veggies you're eating, or you can cool the soup for 10 minutes, pour the mixture into a blender, and pureé until the soup is smooth. Reheat and eat. Serves 4.

Lentil Chili

Lentils are tiny flat seeds that pack a wallop of fiber. Lentils cook in 20 to 30 minutes without prior soaking.

- 1/2 pound lentils
- 5 cups water
- 1/2 teaspoon salt (or to taste)
- 1 large onion, chopped
- 1 bay leaf
- 1 clove garlic, peeled and minced
- 1/2 pound lean ground pork or lean ground turkey
- 16 ounces tomato sauce
- 10 ounces tomato juice
- 8 ounces cold water
- 1 or 2 tablespoons chili powder

Rinse lentils in a colander. Put in large covered pan with bay leaf and water. Bring lentils to a boil, reduce heat, and simmer for 30 minutes. Drain water. Brown the ground pork or turkey with onion, garlic, and salt. Combine the meat mixture with drained lentils. Add tomato sauce, tomato juice, water, and chili powder. Cook for 1 hour to blend flavors.

Coping with PMS (Premenstrual Syndrome)

Crustless Quiche
Try this crustless quiche for breakfast, lunch, or dinner.

    1 tablespoon onion, chopped
    3/4 cup grated Monterey Jack cheese or cheddar cheese
    1 1/2 cup skim milk
    3/4 cup egg product (or 3 eggs)
    1/4 teaspoon dry mustard
    1/2 teaspoon black pepper
    Nonstick vegetable spray

Spray nonstick vegetable oil on the bottom and sides of 8-inch or 9-inch glass pie pan or dish. Mix quiche ingredients together. Then add any of the following vegetables or a mixture of them, up to 1/2 cup: sliced mushrooms, broccoli, cauliflower, diced potatoes, zucchini, red or green bell peppers. Bake at 350°F for about 40 minutes or until set. Serves 4.

Milk, Yogurt, and Cheese

Red, White, and Blueberry Smoothie
This recipe is an adaptation of a recipe from the California Milk Advisory Board.

    1 cup blueberry yogurt
    1 cup sliced strawberries
    1 cup skim milk
    6 ice cubes

Put all of the ingredients into a blender and blend.

Healthy Recipes for Busy Young Women

"Any Fruit" Smoothie
　　1 6-ounce container of yogurt with fruit (if you want to limit your sugar, use plain yogurt)
　　1 cup of a matching fruit (for example, if you use peach yogurt, add fresh, canned, or frozen peaches)
　　1/2 cup skim milk

Throw all of the ingredients into a blender and blend them together until the mixture is smooth.

Fresh Fruit Smoothie
　　1 ripe banana, frozen, if possible
　　1/2 cup fresh strawberries, peaches, or apricots
　　1 cup plain yogurt
　　1/2 cup skim milk

Mix all of the ingredients together in a blender and blend them together until the mixture is smooth.

Camilla's Cheese Squares
Camilla adapted this recipe from the original Green Chile Bites, which appeared in the Junior League of Denver's 1978 cookbook, *Colorado Cache*. It's so easy to make that she takes it to any event that requires guests to bring a snack.

　　1 1/2 cups egg product (or 6 eggs)
　　4 cups (about 1 pound) sharp cheddar cheese, grated
　　1 4-ounce can mild green chiles, chopped and drained
　　Nonstick spray

Spray the bottom and sides of an 8-inch by 8-inch or 9-inch by 9-inch baking dish. Spread green chiles on the bottom of the dish. Sprinkle with grated cheese. Pour the egg product over cheese and chiles. Bake at 350°F for about 30 minutes or until firm. Cut into squares and serve warm.

Fats, Oils, and Sweets

Basic Dressing #1
   1/2 cup olive oil
   1/4 cup balsamic vinegar
   1/2 teaspoon salt
   1/2 teaspoon black pepper
   1/2 teaspoon mustard
   1 teaspoon minced garlic

Combine all the ingredients in a jar with a tight-fitting cover. Shake well. Use the mixture to coat salad greens lightly. Store any leftover dressing in the refrigerator.

Basic Dressing #2
   1/2 cup olive oil
   1/4 cup lemon or lime juice
   1 teaspoon minced garlic
   2 tablespoons oregano
   1/4 teaspoon salt
   1/4 teaspoon pepper

Combine all of the ingredients in a jar and shake. Store leftovers in a refrigerator.

Healthy Recipes for Busy Young Women

Pumpkin Raisin Bread
1 1/2 cups canned pumpkin puree
1/2 cup honey or sugar
1/2 cup melted butter
2 eggs, slightly beaten, or egg product
1/2 cup raisins
1/2 cup walnuts, chopped
1 cup flour
1/2 cup fine yellow cornmeal
1/2 cup rolled oats
1 teaspoon baking powder
1/2 teaspoon ground cinnamon
1/2 teaspoon ground allspice
1/4 teaspoon ground nutmeg
1/4 teaspoon ground ginger
1/4 teaspoon ground cloves
1/2 teaspoon salt
1/2 cup milk

Preheat oven to 350°F. In a medium-sized bowl, mix the pumpkin, honey, melted butter, and eggs or egg product. Stir in milk, raisins, and walnuts. In another bowl, mix the dry ingredients together. Slowly pour in the pumpkin mixture and mix until ingredients are blended. Do not overwork the batter. Pour the batter into a well-greased 6-inch by 9-inch loaf pan. Bake for one hour. Let cool for 10 minutes before cutting.

You can find (or invent) more healthy recipes to add to those in this chapter. You might even want to get a notebook or a recipe file and start your own collection of recipes to help you cope with PMS.

Coping with PMS (Premenstrual Syndrome)

Learning to Live with PMS

Whether you suffer from mild or severe PMS symptoms, you have learned that PMS is a manageable problem. Unlike other illnesses, PMS is difficult to diagnose. When you break a bone, an X ray shows the fracture. When you cut yourself, you bleed. But PMS symptoms can be vague. Many women have a hard time finding a doctor who will listen to their concerns with a serious and caring ear. Nevertheless, it can be done.

If you are like most people, you probably want others to know how you feel. If you have PMS, you have to figure out what makes you feel good, and then do it. You may explain to someone how you are feeling, and find that person not to be as helpful or understanding as you would like. However, following some of the suggestions in this book will help your symptoms and help you take control over your life. The benefits of dealing with your PMS through a healthy lifestyle, anger management, improved communication skills, and possible counseling will not only relieve your symptoms but give you skills to improve all facets of your life.

Glossary

adhesions Abnormal scar tissue that sometimes causes body organs to stick together.
areola Circle of dark skin in the middle of the breast.
breast self-examination (BSE) Technique women use to examine their breasts for suspicious lumps.
certified nurse midwife (CNM) Nurse with specialized training (and certification) in all areas of pregnancy and birthing.
cervix Lower part of the uterus, which protrudes into the upper part of the vagina.
clitoris Female organ at the front of the vulva that is very sensitive to sexual stimulation.
complex carbohydrates Group of foods that includes fruits, vegetables, cereals, grains, pasta, and legumes.
dysmenorrhea Painful menstruation.
embryo Early stage of a developing fetus in humans—from the attachment of the fertilized egg to the uterine wall until about the eighth week of pregnancy.
endometriosis Condition in which the tissue ordinarily lining the uterus appears in other parts of the body, such as the abdominal cavity.

endometrium Lining of the uterus.
estrogen One of two female hormones produced by the ovaries.
fallopian tubes Tubes on each side of the uterus; also called oviducts or egg tubes.
fertilization Entrance of the sperm into the egg; can also be done in the laboratory (in vitro fertilization).
fetus The later stage of a developing infant from the third month of pregnancy.
fibroadenomas Harmless breast lumps that tend to occur most often in women under the age of forty.
follicle Unripened egg.
follicle-stimulating hormone (FSH) Pituitary hormone that stimulates the production of follicles in the ovary and the production of estrogen.
fundus Upper area of the uterus.
genes Biologic units of heredity.
gynecology The science and specialty of diseases of the female reproductive tract.
hormones Chemical substances produced by the endocrine glands and secreted into body fluids to effect certain kinds of organ functioning.
hymen Thin membrane that covers (or partially covers) the vaginal opening.
hypothalamus Part of the brain that regulates the activity of the pituitary gland (among other functions).
intercourse (sexual intercourse) Sexual union between two partners.
labia majora External genitals; large lips on each side of the labia minora.
labia minora External genitals; "small lips" on each side of the clitoris and urethra.

Glossary

laparoscope Instrument used for looking into the abdominal cavity and other body cavities; also used for surgery.

legumes Peas and beans, such as lima beans, garbanzos, kidney beans, lentils, and navy beans.

luteal phase Second half of the menstrual cycle after the rupture of the follicle.

luteinizing hormone (LH) Pituitary hormone that stimulates the production of progesterone.

mammary glands Small glands along with their associated tubules that produce milk in the breast.

masturbation Self-stimulation of sexual organs.

menopause Time of a woman's life when her periods stop, sometime between the ages of forty and fifty-five.

menstrual cycle Monthly cycle including the making of hormones, the thickening of the uterine lining, the shedding of the uterine lining, and menstruation (bleeding).

menstruation Monthly bleeding, sometimes called a period.

mons (also mons pubis or mons veneris) Fleshy area over the joining of the pubic bones (pubic symphysis).

nurse practitioner Nurse with extra training in various medical specialties.

orgasm Peak and release of sexual tension.

ovaries Two female organs that contain eggs (ova).

pelvic inflammatory disease (PID) Infection often caused by sexually transmitted germs that spreads from the uterus to other internal female organs.

peritoneum Abdominal cavity.

pituitary gland Small endocrine gland near the brain that secretes numerous hormones.

premenstrual syndrome (PMS) Group of physical and emotional symptoms that recur in a cyclic manner in the luteal phase of the menstrual cycle.

progesterone Female hormone produced just before ovulation.

psychiatrist Medical doctor with specialized training in mental and emotional disorders.

psychologist Counselor with a master's degree, Psy.D., or Ph.D.

psychotherapy Generally refers to talking therapy.

puberty Period of rapid physical, hormonal, and emotional change that occurs in young women between the ages of ten and sixteen; puberty occurs somewhat later in young men.

pubic region In both males and females, the area at the top of and between the legs.

reproductive organs Body parts involved with pregnancy.

triglycerides Fats in the bloodstream.

urethra Short, thin tube extending from the bladder to the outside of the body to release urine.

uterus Hollow organ with thick walls that expands during pregnancy to accommodate the baby.

vagina Expansive "tube" through which menstrual blood flows or a baby travels to exit the body; sometimes called the birth canal.

vulva External genitals of a female.

womb Another name for the uterus.

Where to Go for Help

If you or someone you know has PMS, the following organizations may be of help. Most provide educational brochures and some will refer you to local resources.

In the United States

American College of Obstetricians and Gynecologists
409 Twelfth Street SW
P.O. Box 96920
Washington, DC 20090-6920
(202) 638-5577
Web site: http://www.acog.org

Institute for Mental Health Initiatives
2175 K Street NW, Suite 700
Washington, DC 20037
(202) 467-2285
e-mail: imhi-info@gwumc.edu
Web site: http://www.gwumc.edu

National Institute of Child Health and Human
    Development (NICHD)
Building 31, Room 2A32, MSC 2425
31 Center Drive
Bethesda, MD 20892-2425
(800) 370-2943

e-mail: NICHDClearinghouse@mail.nih.gov
Web site: http://www.nichd.nih.gov

National Institute of Mental Health
6001 Executive Boulevard
Room 8184, MSC 9663
Bethesda, MD 20892-9663
(301) 443-4513
e-mail: nimhinfo@nih.gov
Web site: http://www.nimh.nih.gov

National Organization for Women
733 15th Street NW, 2nd Floor
Washington, DC 20005
(202) 628-8669
e-mail: now@now.org
Web site: http://www.now.org

National Women's Health Network
514 Tenth Street NW, Suite 400
Washington, DC 20004
(202) 628-7814 (health information)
Web site: http://www.womenshealthnetwork.org

Planned Parenthood Federation of America
Educational Resources
810 Seventh Avenue
New York, NY 10019
(800) 230-7526
(212) 541-7800
e-mail: communications@ppfa.org
Web site: http://www.plannedparenthood.org

Where to Go for Help

U.S. Department of Health and Human Services
Public Health Service
200 Independence Avenue SW
Washington, DC 20201
(877) 696-6775
(202) 619-0257
e-mail: hhsmail@os.dhhs.gov
Web site: http://www.os.dhhs.gov

Women's Health America PMS Access Newsletter
429 Gammon Place
P.O. Box 259690
Madison, WI 53725
(800) 222-4PMS (4767)
e-mail: wha@womenshealth.com
Web site: http://www.womenshealth.com

In Canada

Canadian Research Institute for the Advancement of Women
151 Slater Street, Suite 408
Ottawa, ON K1P 5H3
(613) 563-0681
e-mail: info@criaw-icref.ca
Web site: http://www.criaw-icref.ca

Health Canada
A.L. 0904A
Ottawa, ON K1A 0K9
(613) 957-2991
Web site: http://www.hc-sc.gc.ca

For Further Reading

Boston Women's Health Book Collective. *Our Bodies, Ourselves for the New Century: A Book by and for Women.* New York: Simon & Schuster, 1998.

Brody, Jane. *Jane Brody's Good Food Book: Living the High-Carbohydrate Way.* New York: Bantam Books, 1987.

Cameron, Julia, and Mark Bryan. *The Artist's Way: A Spiritual Path to Higher Creativity.* New York: J. P. Torcher, 1995.

Caudill, Margaret. *Managing Pain Before It Manages You.* New York: Guilford Press, 2001.

Dalton, Katharina, and Wendy Holton. *Once a Month: Understanding and Treating PMS.* Claremont, CA: Hunter House Publishers, 1999.

De Angelis, Lissa G., and Molly Siple. *SOS for PMS: Whole-Food Solutions for Premenstrual Syndrome.* New York: Plume, 1999.

Hahn, Linaya. *PMS: Solving the Puzzle: Sixteen Causes of PMS and What to Do About It.* Evanston, IL: Chicago Spectrum Press, 1995.

Harrison, Michelle, and Marla Ahlgrimm. *Self-Help for Premenstrual Syndrome.* 3rd ed. New York: Random House, 1998.

For Further Reading

Kahaner, Ellen. *Everything You Need to Know About Growing Up Female.* New York: The Rosen Publishing Group, Inc., 2001.

Kallins, George J., and Gloria Keeling. *5 Steps to a PMS Free Life.* Laguna Niguel, CA: Village Healer Press, 2000.

Madaras, Lynda, and Area Madaras. *The What's Happening to My Body? Book for Girls.* New York: Newmarket Press, 2000.

Mitchell, Deborah. *Natural Medicine for PMS.* New York: Dell Publishing Co., 1998.

Owen, Lara. *Honoring Menstruation: A Time of Self-Renewal.* Freedom, CA: Crossing Press, 1998.

Rapkin, Andrea J., and Diana Tonnessen. *PMS: A Woman Doctor's Guide.* New York: Kensington Publishing Corp., 2000.

Skinner, Ilsa Glanzberg, and Denise Skinner. *The PMS Pantry Cookbook.* Los Angeles, CA: LRN Publishing, 1998.

Stengler, Angela, and Mark Stengler. *Natural Solutions for PMS: Top Herbal Remedies and More.* Birmingham, AL: IMPAKT Communications, Inc., 1998.

Vliet, Elizabeth Lee, M.D. *Screaming to Be Heard! Hormonal Connections Women Suspect—and Doctors Still Ignore.* New York: M. Evans and Co., Inc., 2000.

Index

A
acupressure, 90
acupuncture, 90
Ahlgrimm, Marla, 33
anger, 95–99
antianxiety medications, 89–90
antidepressants, 26, 88–90

B
birth control pills, 87
breasts, 4, 8–13
    breast self-exams, 8–12, 79

C
certified nurse midwife (CNM), 78
cervix, 16, 80
clitoris, 13, 15
cognitive distortions, 59–60
counselors, 98, 101
cramps, 14, 18, 25, 37–38

D
Dalton, Dr. Katharina, 26
dandelion, 85
depression, 30, 40–41, 95
diuretics, 88
dong quai, 86
dysmenorrhea, 37–39

E
endometrium, 18, 38
endometriosis, 38
exercise, 52–53
    biking, 54
    cross-country skiing, 54
    jogging, 55

F
fallopian tubes, 15, 17–19, 38–39

G
ginkgo, 85
gynecologist, 78

H
Hippocrates, 26
homeopathy, 90–91
hormones, 4, 6–7
    aldosterone, 28
    estrogen, 4, 6, 18, 28
    follicle-stimulating hormone (FSH), 6, 18
    luteinizing hormone (LH), 6, 18
    progesterone, 4, 6–7, 19, 28, 30, 87–88
    prolactin, 28
hymen, 15
hypothalamus, 4, 6

Index

I
intercourse, 14

L
labia majora, 13
labia minora, 13
laparoscope, 39

M
masturbation, 14
menopause, 20
menstrual cycle, 17, 19, 25, 27
menstrual period, 3, 6, 14, 17, 19–20, 25
menstruation, 7, 17, 19–20
mons pubis, 14

N
National Organization for Women (NOW), 100
nurse practitioner, 78
nutrition, 30, 42–43, 105–108
    alcohol, 47
    caffeine, 44
    complex carbohydrates, 48–49
    fat, 46–47
    grains, 50–51
    nuts, 51–52
    overeating, 48
    vegetables, 49–50

O
ovaries, 4, 16, 18
ovulation, 17–19

P
pain medication, 86–87
pelvic exam, 80
pelvic inflammatory disease (PID), 39
pelvic pain syndrome, 39–40
pituitary gland, 4, 6, 18
pregnancy, 19, 38
premenstrual dysphoric disorder (PMDD), 7, 33, 87
premenstrual syndrome (PMS)
    causes, 28
    cures, 32
    definition, 27
    symptoms, 27–33, 74
    treatment, 2
psychiatrist, 100, 102
psychologist, 100, 102

R
reflexology, 91

S
sleep, 56
stress, 58
support groups, 103

T
tampons, 21–23
therapeutic touch, 91
therapists, 99–100, 102
toxic shock syndrome (TSS), 22–23

U
uterus, 15–19, 38, 80

V
vagina, 13, 15–16, 80
vitamins, 82–85
vulva, 13

About the Author

Barbara Moe has a bachelor of science degree in nursing from the College of Nursing and Health, University of Cincinnati, and a master of science degree in nursing from Ohio State University. She received a master of social work degree, as well as a certificate in marriage and family therapy from the University of Denver. She is the author of several other books for the Rosen Publishing Group, including *Coping with Eating Disorders*, *Coping with Chronic Illness*, *Coping with Mental Illness*, and *Coping with Rejection*.

Layout
Nelson Sá

www.ingramcontent.com/pod-product-compliance
Lightning Source LLC
Chambersburg PA
CBHW052052070526
44584CB00017B/2141